7–

The MAN Whisperer

A Gentle, Results-Oriented Approach to Communication

DONNA SOZIO
and SAMANTHA BRETT

Aadamsmedia

AVON, MASSACHUSETTS

Published by
Adams Media, a division of F+W Media, Inc.
57 Littlefield Street, Avon, MA 02322. U.S.A.
www.adamsmedia.com

ISBN 10: 1-4405-0398-2
ISBN 13: 978-1-4405-0398-6
eISBN 10: 1-4405-0922-0
eISBN 13: 978-1-4405-0922-3

Printed in the United States of America.

10   9   8   7   6   5   4   3   2   1

Library of Congress Cataloging-in-Publication Data
Sozio, Donna.
The man whisperer / Donna Sozio and Samantha Brett.
p. cm.
Includes index.
ISBN-13: 978-1-4405-0398-6
ISBN-13: 978-1-4405-0922-3 (ebk)
ISBN-10: 1-4405-0398-2
ISBN-10: 1-4405-0922-0 (ebk)
1. Man-woman relationships. 2. Communication. I. Brett, Samantha. II. Title.
HQ801.S6765 2011
646.7'8—dc22
2010038812

This book is available at quantity discounts for bulk purchases.
For information, please call 1-800-289-0963.

To our mothers, the ultimate Man Whisperers.

DISCLAIMER

No men were harmed in the writing of this book—we promise!

This book is a collective set of opinions from our experience and expertise and is not meant to be perceived as clinical or doctoral advice. We do not purport to be doctors or psychologists; rather, we offer our opinions about what works today to create fabulous relationships. All names and identifying details have been changed in the illustrative and composite stories and case studies in this book.

This book is not meant to take the place of a licensed professional. If you feel you are in need of medical or psychological advice regarding your personal relationships, we encourage you to take care of yourself and get the help that you need.

CONTENTS

PART 4
Whispering for Great Sex and Attraction That Lasts!

INTRODUCTION

Do you wish your man would open up more about his feelings, conquer his commitment-phobia, be more generous and more affectionate, wax his unibrow, stop scarfing bacon burgers, propose already, take you on a romantic weekend getaway, tell you he loves you more often, and surprise you with flowers . . . just "because"?

Of course you do!

And why?

Because you love him. Unfortunately, thanks to Mr. Darcy, Mr. Big, Dr. McDreamy, and all those other "Mr. Perfect" heroes in Cinderella-like tales, women have been duped. We've spent our entire lives being told that when we meet Mr. Right, he'll fall madly in love with us, put a sparkling ring on our finger—and he'll also clean up after himself, dote on us, romance us, remember to call when he's going to be late (yet again), and that everything will be roses and chocolate-dipped strawberries for all eternity. But no such luck. Suddenly, Mr. Wonderful is not so perfect after all. He needs serious alterations—and fast—before you lose your mind.

If this scenario sounds familiar, you're not alone. The good news is that we've found a way for you to get what you want from your man and your relationship. Welcome to a new method of communication: Man Whispering.

The key to changing the course of your relationship starts and stops with you and the words you use to communicate with your man. Learning to Man Whisper means that you have to start to think, speak, and act differently than you have been in the past and the payoff is that Man Whispering actually gets your man to do the things you've always wanted him to do, all the while getting him to think it was his brilliant idea to do so all along!

In a desperate attempt to make our boyfriends, fiancés, or husbands more like the "Mr. Perfect" we thought we were committing to, many women pick up the nasty habits of nagging, demanding, cajoling, and more nagging in order to get our men to do what we want them to do. The result? Not what we thought it would be. It turns out (surprise!) that nagging does not get our men off the couch and springing into action. Instead nagging only results in men looking for *more* excuses to escape from us and honestly, who can blame them? Nagging makes a man feel like he is a loser who can't do a damn thing right . . . not your Prince Charming. And nagging only leads you to become yet another disillusioned woman taking out the garbage herself and wondering what the heck is wrong with her man. Nag and nobody wins!

Yet when you learn how to Man Whisper, fairy tales do come true. You'll have your man eating out of the palm of your hand and you'll be lavished with his time and attention in the most generous ways—without begging, resentment, or backlash. (It's true!)

In fact, it's actually within a man's DNA to behave like the dreamboat you've always wanted him to be—you just need to learn how to bring it out of him. Men actually want to fix things, take care of you, be your knight in shining armor, clean the pool (probably not in a Speedo, but hey, Man Whispering has been known to get men to do just about anything to please women), fix the sink, and do whatever it is you request of them. Why? Because men *want* to please you.

The good news is that Man Whispering doesn't involve complicated strategies, intimidating theories, games, or manipulation. Instead it's simply a shift in your perspective and in the words you use, how you phrase them, and the way you lay out requests. You'll love it, and he will too—we guarantee it. And after you learn the methods in this book, we promise that other women will corner you in bars and stalk you on the street wanting to learn your secrets with men. Because when you learn how to whisper to his mind, body, and spirit, a man wants to make you happy the way you always dreamed a man would.

So whether you're dating a new man, are in a long-term relationship, are hitched, or fall somewhere in between, you can start Man Whispering right now. In fact, it can turn your relationship around—no matter how far south or sour you fear it's gone. You'll start enjoying the benefit of a more balanced and complementary romantic relationship that you've long wished for.

So what are you waiting for? Read on ... and start whispering!

PART 1

Whispering to

Relationship Bliss

CHAPTER 1

The Man Whisperer Method

Five steps to getting what you want from a man (every single time!)

"The only time a woman really succeeds in changing a man is when he is a baby."
—NATALIE WOOD

"You can't change a man. But a man can change!"
—DONNA AND SAM

What Is Man Whispering?

Man Whispering is a new way of communicating with men that makes them want to turn off the TV, tell their buddies "next time!" when they're invited to a poker game, and put down that beer to give you their full attention. Finally he will no longer think of you as his ball and chain. Instead, you'll become his beloved girlfriend, wife, or fiancée. He'll be genuinely excited to spend the rest of his life with you, dote on you, want to listen to you in a caring, thoughtful way!

> **Man Whisperer:** A super-subspecies of the female gender who has learned (through trial and error) to adopt a sympathetic view of her man's motives, needs, and desires. She effectively negotiates a win-win resolution while using imperceptible key buzzwords, which inspire her man to satisfy her requests, all the while making it seem like *his* brilliant idea.

Learning to whisper to your man sets your relationship in the direction of love, peace, and fulfillment rather than on a path filled with frustration, mistrust, and a constant, painstaking rerun of the same old fights and disappointments. Best of all, whispering is not about manipulation, lies, or demands.

Instead, it is a refined art of getting a man to do what you want him to do by getting him to think his new behavior is all his brilliant idea!

COUPLES CASE STUDY: HEIDI AND JAMES

Thirty-six-year-old Heidi has been married to James for three years. She describes her husband as "useless" (and isn't afraid to tell him so!). She nags him nonstop. The two of them are at each other's throats over the smallest things. In Heidi's eyes, he never seems to get off his butt to help her with the groceries or take her out for a romantic dinner. Heidi feels that most of the time he's too busy watching sports to have a heart-to-heart about how their relationship is going. And then, after sitting on the couch all night, James gets into bed, gives her leg a pat, and wants sex! Silently she's been stewing, building up resentment and harboring unspoken anger. Certainly, their relationship wasn't always this way. But over the years, Heidi has felt like they weren't equal partners and that James wasn't pulling his fair share of the weight. Heidi didn't like to nag. It didn't make her feel good. But she thought it was the only way to get James to do anything.

Because Heidi feels that she and James need to be equals in the relationship, she engages in silent score-keeping. When the numbers aren't equal, resentments and tempers rise. In many relationships where this is the case, women don't feel appreciated because usually she's the one doing "more." But what Heidi has yet to realize is that if she stops keeping score (trying to be equals) in her romantic relationship and starts whispering about her appreciation of all that her husband does (which is more than she thinks!) their relationship has the potential to become the marriage she always dreamed of.

Heidi blamed their relationship problems on the fact that they had just become too busy—she felt like they were two lonely ships passing in the night. Heidi was in a prestigious MBA program and James was up for a promotion and working overtime. Because home had become a war zone, James would hit the gym after work or go for a beer with his work buddies. To avoid conflict or feeling lonely, Heidi headed out for cocktails with the girls or zoned out at yoga. Neither one wanted to give up what felt like the only pleasure of their day to spend it with someone who was uptight, frazzled, and grumpy. Heidi longed for the days when they had what felt like electricity running through them and they could talk for hours. Now, it seemed that James didn't have two minutes and she had to fight to even get that.

One night, when James forgot to get what Heidi needed at the grocery store (again), she went right in with her usual, "You never do anything for me; remind me why we are in this relationship anyway?" knockout tirade. Her intent was to get James to simply pay some attention to her! Feeling neglected, Heidi barked (as she often did) at James for not listening when she asked him to do something, for not spending enough time with her, for never telling her that he loved her anymore, and for treating her like the maid rather than the hot girlfriend he romanced and married! James reacted defensively, stating that he had a lot on his mind with work and that she was always at his throat anyway so it's not like he could do anything right as it was. "Why should I bother?" he responded. What followed was the usual heated argument. They didn't talk for three days, sex was out of the question, and they grew more distant. James resented Heidi's silent treatment. Heidi resented that James wasn't showing her the love and affection she hoped he would. And both of them were miserable, disillusioned, and wondering what the hell was wrong with their relationship—and all of this was because of the darn groceries!

None of Heidi's unhappiness was actually because of the groceries. It was all due to the invisible, silent accounting system that she used to keep track of who was doing what in the relationship . . . rather than to create a complementary relationship in which they divide the tasks and each does what they do best. Certainly, Heidi could learn to whisper to her man and turn it all around. She needed to start to learn how to use a new feminine communication style that would allow her to communicate to her man in a way that he feels good responding to.

What Man Whispering Can Do for Your Relationship
The art of Man Whispering:

- Creates a harmonious relationship with your partner, devoid of petty arguments or constant nagging.
- Creates a dynamic team between you and your man and gives you the mentality and strength to enable you to truly believe that you can do anything together.

- Makes communicating with your man seamless, easy, enjoyable, and devoid of stress—no matter what the topic or the situation.
- Will create a more romantic, doting, loving man who will not be afraid to express his romantic side with you more often.
- Will bring "sexy" back into your sex life.

No matter how distant things have become between you and your man, and no matter what stage of the relationship you are in, you hold the key to turning things around for the better.

Man Whispering in Five Easy Steps

Practicing these five simple steps will help you develop an inner awareness so that you'll be able to whisper intuitively and successfully to your man. And don't fret that you're going to have to think too hard every time you open your mouth. The process will eventually become second nature. Learning this new type of communication is part art and part science, and we'll be diving right into the biology behind it (by analyzing your man's brain in Chapter 4) so you'll understand how and why it all works. Once you get past the initial learning curve, Man Whispering will become your default communication style with your man—and you'll see his transformation to Mr. Wonderful before you know it!

Suddenly, life will seem just that much easier. You'll be pushing less, not nagging, and yet you'll get him to get more done. You'll use a different tone to get what you want, and it will seem effortless. Why? Because Man Whispering doesn't force either one of you to paddle upstream. It's a communication style that complements the natural flow between men and women and brings out the best in each.

So how do you whisper to your man? We've broken it down into five simple steps.

Step 1: Identify the Issue

Before you begin communicating with your man, you need to figure out what you want to talk about. This may sound obvious, but many women jump into conversations by talking about some insignificant, nitpicky issue rather than what's *really* bothering them. That tactic annoys men and doesn't get you what you want anyway! We've identified five common types of issues that women want to talk about with men and chances are, the topic on your mind falls into one of these categories:

- Wanting your man to talk about something that is bothering you
- Wanting your man to talk about something that is bothering him
- Wanting your man to fix something—e.g., the broken sink, the running toilet, the computer
- Wanting your man to do something—e.g., walk the dog, hang out with your friends more often, clean the garage
- Wanting your man to give you something—e.g., a back rub, an orgasm, a deeper commitment

Once you've identified the issue, try to understand why you want it from him. Is it simply utilitarian, like doing the dishes after dinner because that's a chore you really hate? Or does it run deeper—you want him to do the dishes because you currently do *everything* and are feeling underappreciated as a result? Once you pinpoint the underlying emotional need for your request, you will be more able to communicate it and find just the right words to whisper.

Step 2: Pose the Issue Effectively

Once you identify what you desire and why you want it, the next step is to phrase it to your man in a way that is a request, observation, or question with a benefit that guides and inspires him to take action. Make sure to let him know what's in it for him (the benefit) . . . . and most often, that in itself is enough to get him to act. It's important to note that this isn't bribery. It's simply reminding him that when you're happy . . . he's happy. Whispering to your man is always win/win!

Make sure that the benefits you add into your Man Whispering formula are the things that motivate men: food, peace and quiet, a "hall pass" to bond with his buddies, shiny new objects, and sex.

ALERT! *Forget about Hints*

Whispering is not about dropping "hints" and then getting frustrated when men can't read your mind. This is a mind reading-free zone!

Here are some examples of how to phrase a request:

- "Would you (insert intended action) . . . + the benefit?"
- "Would you mind (insert intended action) . . . + the benefit?"
- "What do you think about (insert intended action/ request/desire) . . . + the benefit?"

- "Would you ever consider (insert intended action/request/desire) . . . + the benefit?"
- "I was hoping that (insert intended action/request/desire) . . . + the benefit."
- "I would love if (insert intended action) . . . + the benefit."
- "I would very much like (insert need/request/desire) . . . + the benefit."
- "What about (insert intended action) or (insert need/request/desire) . . . + the benefit?"
- "How about (insert intended action) or (insert need/request/desire) . . . + the benefit?"

Here's the difference between Man Whispering . . . and not:

- "How about going to (intended action) our favorite Italian place tonight? I know you love the rigatoni with cream sauce they have . . ." *Not* . . . "You never take me out for dinner, you cheapskate!"
- "How about getting down and doing the dirty tonight?" *Not* . . . "You're always too tired for sex. What's wrong with you?!"
- "Babe, I'm in a party mood (observation). How about I put on a sexy outfit (benefit for him) and we go dancing (suggestion)?" *Not* . . . "I hate always staying at home on the couch. You suck!"
- "How about sprucing up (request) our backyard today so you can have your friends over for a barbeque (benefit)?" *Not* . . . "We need to get rid of those damn weeds!"
- "How about I pay this stack of bills and you go down on me tonight?" *Not* . . . "I'm sick of paying all these damn bills and I'm never satisfied in the bedroom!"

Compliments Go a Long Way

Offering compliments is a great way to initiate request/benefit statements. You want to pack in as many genuine compliments and positives as you can without sounding (or feeling!) like a parrot. Many observations can serve as compliments too. A great Man Whispering combination is Compliment—Suggestion—Compliment. That way you always begin and end on a high note.

For example:

- "Have you been doing pushups? Your arms look so hard and amazing! (compliment) Can you use those big muscles to move my boxes of winter clothes up to the attic? (request) They're super-heavy but I know you're strong enough to carry them. (compliment)"
- "Wow, you are so good in bed! (compliment) Oh, just a little to the left (request) . . . yes, that's right . . . you're such a natural! (compliment)"

You can lead with a compliment even when your main need/request/desire is for him to work out at the gym more because he's getting jiggly around the belly. By complimenting him on one body part, he'll want to please you by getting the others in shape as well. Likewise, by complimenting him on one room in his apartment that looks presentable and gently making an observation about the others, you'll get him to want to clean/improve the rest!

Using Casual Observations

Besides compliments, presenting simple observations is an effective way to gently introduce a request. (Again, no nagging!) Here are some examples of observations:

- "Looks like (insert observation) . . . ."
- "Is it just me, or (insert observation) . . . ."
- "Oh, your Xs are getting so Y . . . ."
- "That's a (insert description) . . ."
- "What a (insert description) . . ."
- "I've been reading about (insert need/request/desire) . . ."
- "I just heard that (insert observation) . . ."
- "I'm so (insert feeling) but there's no (insert observation) . . ."
- "I feel like (insert need/request/desire) . . ."
- "I just read an article about how eating fish is good for your health (observation). Think we should try a seafood meal once a week instead of our burger night? (request)"
- "I just heard that a hot new tapas restaurant opened up downtown (observation). Think we should try it sometime? (request)"
- "Looks like it's going to be a gorgeous day outside (observation). A trip to the beach might be nice. What do you think? (request)"
- "Is it just me, or is there a really bad smell coming from the garbage bin?" (observation)

Step 3: Zip It!

When there's a silence in a serious conversation with your man, do you find yourself immediately filling it with your preconceived solutions to the problem at hand? Your man's eyes probably glaze over as he tunes you out and starts rolling his eyes or glancing at the clock. It's time to start enjoying the silence as you instead embrace Step 3 of Man Whispering: Zip It!

"Zipping It" is a great way of saving your precious breath and leaving a little time for the man in your life to come up with a viable solution to the "dilemma" you presented to him. Men don't process thoughts as fast as women do (or so it seems!), and it takes them a few moments or hours to come up with a solution. To do so effectively, men need silence. Your man may even need to retreat back to his man cave for a little while—so let him.

When you leave a healthy silence (definitely no nagging!), your man will come up with the solution sooner—and chances are, you'll like it better than if you had just kept talking, talking, and talking. Little moments of silence work magic on a man. Once you make a request, stop talking. Learn to let him fill the space with a solution.

Step 4: Let *Him* Fix It

Men by nature are natural fixers—they generally think more systematically than women, and they like working through problems. Instead of spoon-feeding your man a solution you think would work well, let him fix whatever issue you brought up in Step 1. This allows him to feel like your knight in shining armor—no matter how simple the solution is. Plus, he's more likely to be committed to the solution if he was responsible for creating it. You may even be surprised at his creativity, passion, and dedication—all of which you'll probably see when you step back and let him take the lead.

Step 5: Reward Him for Fixing the Problem

You know that saying, "No good deed goes unpunished"? Well, that was coined by men whose women nag them. When you whisper to a man, don't leave out this step—especially if it's a small deed. Always let him know how much you appreciated what he just did for you. Rewards can be a kiss on the cheek, a smile, a squeeze on the arm, or simply kind words letting him know that what he did made you happy.

There's another way to look at appreciation: growth. You want your investments (good things in your relationship) to appreciate (grow). So appreciating his good deeds even when they are small ensures that they will grow in number and in scope!

Your showing genuine appreciation is just one of the reasons this communication technique works so well. When men offer solutions to your problems, they are showing you who they are deep down. It's an intimate act, which is one of the things women crave. And when you appreciate who they are and the fact that they're offering up solutions because they love you and they're showing their inner selves, you get more of the best of them.

Because men show you who they are by what they offer to give to you, it can be very painful for them when you belittle their solutions. When women are unappreciative, men feel rejected. When they are appreciated, they feel loved and therefore share more love with you.

Whispering Brings Out the Best in Men

Once you start whispering effectively, you may notice some changes in your man: He's more giving, cooperative, and thoughtful. But it's important to remember that *you* didn't change him. You simply helped facilitate a transformation that he already had the skill and desire to make. You've inspired your man to please you by showing him that you have faith and trust in his ability to do so. Whispering also inspires men who act more like boys than men (which is mightily frustrating at the best of times) to become great men. And it inspires great men to become even greater.

By simply inspiring him to become his best and allowing him the space to do it, your man will never be resentful, blameful, or think that you're manipulating him in any way, shape, or form. When you gently present a problem, give him the time and space to solve it, and then tell him how much you appreciated his efforts, you're providing a healthy, loving atmosphere for your relationship—and your man—to thrive. Changes in his behavior may happen as a result . . . but he was responsible for them!

Using Feminine Communication

An innate part of Man Whispering is embracing your natural feminine style of communication. It may sound counterintuitive, but *feminine* communication actually brings out the best *masculine* aspects in your man. Rather than demanding and nagging to try to get your man to spring into action (which is using forceful communication—which is actually a masculine communication style!), use feminine communication—which creates flow without force—to leverage your man's innate desire to please you and be the Good Guy.

> **Feminine communication:** Feminine communication is the lost art of speaking to men using a specific tone and specific language to relay your desires, requests, and needs. This specific tone and language inspires a man's genetic wiring to provide for you, please you, and satisfy your desires, requests, and needs.

To get your point across so that men can receive the information (and not just hear the ubiquitous "nag nag nag" sound coming out of your mouth), phrase your request in a way that inspires, observes, suggests, and guides, rather than demands, takes control, limits, and threatens. Feminine communication is the way forward not only in romantic relationships, but also when communicating with men in other situations—like when you take your car to your mechanic—or anytime you want a man to do something for you.

> "In my forty years of marriage, there were definitely times when I felt like biting my husband's head off. But I bit my tongue, smiled sweetly, and moved away from the heated topic or argument. While my friends thought I was 'performing,' I'll tell you, it worked. Those were the best years of my life."
>
> —SILVIA, 82, RETIRED

Feminine Communication in Action

Let's use Heidi and James's relationship as an example of how to implement feminine communication.

Say James came home from work in yet another one of his foul moods. Instead of falling into her automatic negative reaction (rolling her eyes, sighing) or using forceful communication (by making demands on him), Heidi learned to and practiced creating this scenario:

"I was thinking . . . I haven't worn that sexy black dress you like in quite a while. You know, the one that's backless and drops down to there . . ." said Heidi.

"Er, I forgot about it," James replied, a little intrigued.

Heidi then took a step closer, smiled, and gently touched his arm.

"I was hoping I might get a chance to wear it this week," she cooed.

Then she paused and waited for James's response. After what felt like an excruciatingly long four seconds, he replied, "Let me see what I can do."

Heidi put her lips right next to his, made eye contact with him, and whispered in his ear, "I would love that."

Heidi jumped when she received a text from James the following day at lunchtime reading, "How's Nobu Sushi, 8 P.M. Friday?" She immediately texted back, "Thank you sweetie, I'm going to look gorgeous for you!" A few seconds later her phone beeped back. "Love you," he wrote.

This type of communication with your man may seem like a dream. But it's not. Let's break down exactly what Heidi did to achieve the result she wanted.

Don't Make Any Demands

If you noticed, Heidi didn't demand anything. Not a single thing. Nor did she complain. Nor did she try to control the situation by insisting on too many specifics about when, where, and how she wanted to be taken out. She also didn't bulldoze over and belittle him by fixing the situation herself and planning a special night for him that he might see as an obligation.

Give Him One Problem to Solve and Then Zip It

Instead of barraging him with too much information or a hundred requests, Heidi casually gave James *one* single problem to solve. She did this by making a casual observation about her desire to wear a sexy dress. Then she communicated what would be in it for James should he solve her "dilemma" of wanting to be taken out (he would get to see her hot body and get to feel like a major rock star stud with her on his arm). And then Heidi Zipped It. She waited for his answer, and let him speak without interrupting him. Hence, James was given the opportunity to solve the problem on his own, all the while thinking that it was his brilliant idea all along.

Use Persuasive Nonverbal Communication

Heidi's "statements" were a mix of verbal and nonverbal communication. She smiled, letting her husband know that she wasn't angry. She created a loving space within which they could both successfully operate. She also touched him in a sweet way to reinforce that she wasn't going to yell, nag, or punish him for not pleasing her in the past. This nonverbal communication set up a restatement of her request in a positive way that her man's brain could actually compute.

After James offered a solution to her "dilemma," she praised him via text and fluffed his man feathers for coming up with the brilliant idea of taking her to a nice restaurant. This positive reinforcement is a surefire way to bring out his Good Guy mentality more often from now on!

Soften Your Demeanor

Good Guys hate getting in trouble. And when you nag them they immediately feel emasculated—like a little boy with his nose to the chalkboard who got in trouble at school.

Add little openers like "Oh, honey," or "My goodness," before stating the issue, as these soften the blow of the request.

It shows that you are relaxed about it and aren't about to attack your poor man. So feel free to soften! Melt around your edges. This makes your man feel safe to step in and be your hero because he knows he's not in trouble. Relaxing your demeanor allows men to feel confident enough to show you who they are and give you what they have.

Let Him Call the Shots

Remember that part of the underlying wisdom of whispering is setting up your man to be a confident leader in your relationship. He is "calling the shots"; after all, he's the Good Guy! But remember, he is making decisions to please you because you are communicating what you want. It's all about gently pitching him your needs and requests in such a way that he can hit them out of the park for a home run again and again. Mature men want to be heroes when it comes to pleasing you.

Heidi let James choose the day, time, and restaurant. He called those shots. She didn't need to micromanage the date itself; she simply stated her request and let him work out the details. Be prepared to relax and let your man make some decisions.

Be Patient!

It's unwise to expect results from Man Whispering immediately. After all, both you and your partner need to get used to the new style of communication, problem solving, and appreciation. But patience pays off! So gently bring up your needs, wants, and desires over and over again until your man suddenly takes action on what he thinks was his brilliant idea. Eureka! You get what you want.

However, don't be daunted if your man initially disagrees with your suggestion, observation, or request. He might shoot it down or dismiss it; sometimes this is part of the process! The goal is to get him to think the suggestion or request was *his* idea. But when he's new to the process, he doesn't yet have enough practice or confidence to think that way. So keep planting those seeds and making gentle requests. Keep reminding him of the benefits, and why it's in his best interest to please you. Then wait. Usually, the issue will pop up again later and he'll offer the exact same suggestion you made, only now it's his awesome idea. Thank him. And lavish him with affection and appreciation. Trust the process.

Remember, you're giving your man all the information necessary to make a decision with you in mind. Some men know the right questions to ask to glean the information necessary to please you, but most don't. Whispering is about giving them the missing piece and not expecting them to read your mind. That process takes time, so hang in there.

Don't Take the Credit

Even if the solution your man comes up with is exactly what you had suggested, never take credit for it. Ever. It's imperative that you let him think whatever you're proposing was his idea.

What? you say. *I have a great idea and I have to let him take all the credit?* Well, yes. It's a small price to pay for getting what you want. When your husband comes home with a shiny new Volvo for the family, refrain from saying, "So you finally bought the car I've been telling you to get for three years!" Non–Man Whisperers take the wind out of his sails when they say, "That's what *I* said!" Simply smile to yourself and dish the story to your girlfriends over martinis the following night if you must. Remember, there is an element of performance to whispering, which most often includes Zipping It and biting your tongue. Take the high road and appreciate that he came to the same decision as you.

ALERT! **A Man's Take on Communicating**

Our friend Scott Solder, coauthor of *You Need This Book to Get What You Want*, gave us a great suggestion about communicating with men. He says you can get in sync emotionally with your man by matching his mood and getting in the same frame of mind *before* you make your request. You can even mirror his tone or posture. If he's upbeat and happy, act upbeat and happy. If he's mellow and quiet, act the same. Scott says, "It works much better to approach a conversation like this, rather than to just come out with it all at once, out of the blue—especially if you happen to be in different frames of mind at the time."

The Top Ten Man Whisperer Mantras

You're about to be introduced to the basic tenets that you should keep in mind as you begin to create Man Whispering bliss in your relationship. Keep this list in your purse at all times and think of it as your quick reference, instant support, or, if you need it, a quick kick in the butt to get you back onto the Man Whispering path when you feel like you're going astray!

1. **Thou shalt not withhold physical affection from your man.** Don't withhold sex and affection from your man and replace it with the silent treatment, bitchy looks, and rebuffs. You're mightily mistaken if you believe that this behavior will make him suddenly begin doing what you want him to do. On the contrary, he'll become more withdrawn, annoyed, and unwilling to please.

2. **Thou shalt not punish men for meaningless bad behavior.** Forget the doghouse. Reward the good behavior and don't sweat the small stuff. Rather than get worked up about his leaving dirty socks on the floor, just toss them in the laundry and move on.

3. **Thou shalt give up the need to impress men with your achievements.** A man falls in love with your spirit, not the mountains or corporate ladders you've climbed. Don't recite your resume to him—you're looking for a relationship, not a career.

4. **Thou shalt Zip It and let him figure it out.** Your man may need a moment—or a few hours—of silence to think and come up with a plan of action to please you all on his own. You don't need to give him a "helping hand" by solving everything yourself.

5. **Thou shalt never fake an orgasm.** Faking only leads him to mistakenly think he's Casanova and leaves you feeling perpetually unsatisfied. That's a lose-lose situation!

6. **Thou shalt never put a man or your relationship with a man before your safety.** Your safety is paramount, and you shalt not tolerate abuse in any form.

7. **Thou shalt not complain, gossip, or bitch about your man to others.** Kiss and bitch only if you want things to get worse. Otherwise, only let trusted counselors hear all the nitty-gritty details.

8. **Thou shalt not nag your man.** Nagging is the antithesis to Man Whispering and bites you in the butt every time.

9. **Thou shalt always reward his good behavior with respect and appreciation (and meatloaf!).** A healthy reward system lets your man know he's hit the bull's-eye in pleasing you.

10. **Thou shalt not try to change a man.** Instead, love who he is and whisper to bring out his best.

More Man Whispering Mantras
Chapter 1

- At first, learning and implementing the basics of Man Whispering may feel a bit contrived. But remember, it's a process that you make your own as you master it.
- Mix and match the different parts (requests, observations, compliments) in different orders that make sense to you.
- No matter how you go about it, the goal is the same. You want to leverage your man's natural desire to please you and be your hero by allowing him to "fix" your issue or concern. Then appreciate and praise him for it!

Man Whispering Myths and Misconceptions

Ten communication mistakes that can cost you true love (and your sanity!)

"Women have a wonderful instinct about things.
They can discover everything except the obvious."
—OSCAR WILDE

"Obvious is relative."
—DONNA AND SAM

"I'm Not So Sure about This Idea . . ."

Let's get right down to business and address your fears and doubts about Man Whispering. Do you feel like you shouldn't have to change your communication style for a man? That he should respond to your requests, no matter how you present them? And that you should be able to make demands on your man and speak your mind? What about feminism and equal rights? You may be thinking that in this day and age, you've earned the right to have relationships your way! So why should you Zip It, let him fix things on his own, stroke his ego, and then wait for him to do what you wanted?

Quite simply, because it gets you what you want in romantic relationships. That's why. This type of feminine communication speaks to a man's brain so that he can respond to you the way you want him to without him feeling resentful or that he's been played or manipulated. Instead of the constant classic tug-of-war about who is right or wrong, who is doing more or less or whatever the fight du jour is about, use Man Whispering to turn it all around. Unfortunately, with everything from modern technology to feminism changing (and confusing!) the way men and women communicate, effective communication between the sexes has become a lost art—and we are intent on bringing it back!

Most people think in either/or terms. A woman may think that she can either have a happy relationship or be a career woman with unfortunately no time for men. But the beauty of being a Man Whisperer is its "yes, and" mentality. We say, "Yes, I'll have a successful career *and* a fulfilling romantic relationship in a way that enlivens me and keeps me young at heart." Here are some other myths about Man Whispering that we can put to rest right now.

Myth #1: "Man Whispering means I am changing my man."

Unfortunately, it's common for a woman to enter into a relationship with a man thinking he has the potential to become who she wants, rather than accepting him for who he already is. "Women treat men as their pet project," one man told us. Ladies, if you want to lose a guy, then go ahead and treat him as your pet project. But we don't recommend it.

Still, a woman may commit to a relationship under the misconception that she will go about changing him into what pleases her, and only then will she feel confident being in a relationship with him. She may truly believe that with a little dose of her feminine wiles, the man will fall under her spell and magically transform from a bad boy into a nice guy (Sandra Bullock learned her painful lesson!); a fat slob into an iron man; a shy bookworm into an outgoing Casanova. Certainly, after reading this book and putting its principles into practice, it's very likely that your man will change. But we'll repeat it again . . . *you won't change him.* He will change because he wants to keep you. You will let him know what you need from him and he will take the appropriate action to make sure you're happy. That's why Man Whisperers are calm, cool, and collected, not desperate. They know when to Zip It and let him fix it, which biologically (as we'll explain in the coming chapters) is exactly what men are hardwired to do. So let him operate at his best.

Myth #2: "I have to nag him . . . otherwise he'd never do anything!"

If you're still not convinced that nagging doesn't work, perhaps hearing it from men themselves will convince you. Every time we poll men in our Man Whispering roundtables, they all have one similar gripe. It's not the fact that you don't look like Heidi Klum, that you burn their toast, or don't give them enough oral sex. We haven't heard one complaint that their partner's butt is too big or the fact that they're wearing last year's Tory Burch wedges. Nope. The number one issue men continue to vent to us about is nagging. "If she'd just stop nagging me all the time, instead of trying to block her out, I might just do what she asks!" they say, frustrated, forlorn, and defeated.

Nag enough and he'll leave either in his heart and mind or legally, on paper. Nagging makes him think that you're never happy and that it's impossible to satisfy you. Too much nagging and he'll give up on you and the relationship. So, pull the plug. Men don't hear you when you nag anyway.

> **The Nag Zone:** The period during which you demand, cajole, and even bully your man into taking action. This is you in the middle of the Nag Zone—and well out of Man Whispering territory!

There is a way to have your requests met without nagging: whispering!

Myth #3: "Isn't Man Whispering 'Faking It' or Manipulation?"

There's tremendous wisdom in the phrase, "fake it until you make it." There is an element of performance to communicating with men—you should control your actions, reactions, and demeanor, just as a performer would on stage (if you want results!). Your instant reaction isn't always the best action to take, especially in the heat of the moment. When you trade your steely "I can do it myself" persona for a softer persona a man can truly connect with, you might at first feel like you're faking it or putting on an act. But you'll quickly realize major benefits and find that you actually enjoy yourself so much more than you did when you felt like you had to nag or beg. And let's be honest for a minute here, do you really *want* to nag? No! You want to speak lovingly to your man. That's what Man Whispering allows you to do. Instead of sticking to what doesn't work, shake it up and turn around habitual behaviors that aren't serving you. Start acting differently around your man. It's not faking it if you decide you want to improve your behavior and reactions!

ALERT! *Don't Manipulate*

Man Whispering is not about manipulation. Instead, you help and inspire men to do what they are designed to do: come up with solutions, solve problems, provide, and give generously to show their love.

Take twenty-nine-year-old high-flyer Sarah, for example. At work, she is brazen: Top of her sales team, she has a reputation as a fearless cold-caller and stops at nothing to get the best accounts. But as soon as she turns her key in the door at home and she's with her man, Sarah acts like a totally different woman. "I love letting my man lead," she says. "It's like going on vacation. Life is just easier. I don't feel like I have to do everything myself anymore." Sure, he often gets lost and refuses to ask for directions. And yes, his cooking is rather average, but he loves to do it—so she happily compliments his dishes and relishes the fact that he's doing the cooking (and the driving) so she can relax! Find out what his strengths are, and even if he's not the best at something (and you can do it better), it's important to let him lead and allow him the space to do something he enjoys so that he feels good about himself. Focus less on the end result and compliment him on taking the initiative to do things . . . like cook dinner for you! It's perfectly okay to have two different sides of yourself—one that's take-charge in certain circumstances and one that's laid-back in others.

Myth #4: "I can't be a feminist and a Man Whisperer!"

When discussing Man Whispering, we're often asked the question, "Doesn't Man Whispering go against feminism?" Our answer is a definitive "No!" We are both bona fide feminists and know that you can absolutely be a feminist and still reap the benefits of whispering. The trouble we've found is that while feminism did wonders for women in many areas—from the workplace to politics to sex—it also succeeded in mightily confusing the heck out of both the sexes when it comes to modern-day romantic relationships. While women were achieving what they wanted in their careers, many made the mistake of thinking that insisting on equality was also the way to get what they wanted in their romantic lives. Many thought the same behavior and attitudes employed to get a promotion would also bring them love, romance, and a doting husband.

And who could blame us? After all, the experts were sold on the notion, too. Books and articles began popping up telling women to "Think like a man!" "Act like a man!" "Be more masculine!" "Be a bitch!" and "Nice girls finish last!" We were told that if we acted more masculine—ask men out, have sex when we want to, wear the pants, and rule the roost—then we'd get what we wanted.

And that strategy worked, for a little while—well . . . kind of. Pretty soon, men got bored. They became complacent and started using women not only for sex but also a free meal. All the while, women who believed they could have sex "like men" were being duped by their female brain. You see, every time we women get naked between the sheets, we release a little hormone called "oxytocin," which makes us practically fall in love with the guy we just bonked—even if we just met him (and even if he is Mr. I-hope-no-one-finds-out!). If you want to have sex like a man (and there's nothing wrong with a little bedroom action if you are clear in your own mind about your intentions up-front), then go for it! But if you want to have a successful relationship with a man (and not just be his booty-call buddy), focus on being *complementary* to him instead of being so forceful. Successful romantic relationships involve your using feminine communication to bring out your man's masculine qualities—not the other way around! Focus on a complementary union, whereby you respect and embrace each other's differences while growing and learning more about yourself and your mate.

> **Complementary relationships:** The best romantic part-
> nerships are not ones that are equal, but complementary.
> When you are in a complementary relationship, you play
> off each other's strengths and weaknesses rather than try
> to get him to be and feel the same way as you do. Com-
> plementary relationships allow for tremendous freedom
> to be yourself.

Most feminists think of feminism as a belief that they should have what men are entitled to—especially in the workplace. This means equal pay, equal opportunities, and equal respect. But "equality" in romantic relationships is measured in much harder-to-quantify notions of love, mutual respect, and happiness. The key to a successful relationship is that you *both* enjoy all of those notions. Man Whispering helps you use your innate femininity to achieve all those goals so you can feel as happy and relaxed in your relationship as your man does. Neither one of you should feel overworked or underappreciated.

Myth #5: "Man Whispering means I'll become a 'yes' woman."

Absolutely not! This is not about turning into a "yes" woman, or becoming subservient to your man. A "yes" woman puts her man above her own well-being and throws her dreams under the bus to preserve what is usually an unhealthy relationship. "Yes" women undercut themselves to get the man, a com-mitment, and the coveted diamond ring. You see this when women don't make plans "just in case he calls"—then leap out of their skin if he texts at 10 P.M. with a "Hey, how r u." Nor do "yes" women speak up if a man is doing something that makes her feel uncomfortable—like flirting with her friends. Man Whispering is about reclaiming your feminine power. It's about learning how men think and leveraging that information so you can inspire them into action that is free of resentment. ("Yes" women harbor loads of resentment; they are the secret score keepers—you are not!) In relationships, it's imperative to make sure that you're a team and that every situation is a win-win. Man Whispering lets your man feel like he's calling the shots because you're letting him. Not because you can't do it yourself. We know you can. Man Whispering lets him know that you he can, too!

Myth #6: "I need to impress a man to get him to love me."

Ever notice a woman on a date in a restaurant trying so hard to impress a man, while he looks like he's about to nod off and fall face-first into his steak? We've seen it all too often: women bragging on a date about unparalleled feats of bravery, unmatched knowledge in politics, prowess with the wine list, and tales of travels to remote corners of the world.

Seriously, ladies, why out-man the man who hopes that you will look up to him and that he can win your heart with his own stories of bravery and manliness? We are sure that you have extraordinary tales to tell that would make your Twitter followers green with envy. But a new date isn't the time or the place to recount them. Your stories of adventure and accomplishment won't get you what you really want. Why? Because men don't fall in love with accomplishments. A man will fall in love with your inner qualities, like humor, insight, and adorability—not how many times you've been scuba diving with man-eating sharks!

So while you're out with your man, if you catch yourself saying:

"And then I climbed Mt. Kilimanjaro after volunteering at the orphanage just after I saved a baby whale. And you know what I learned? The politics in Zimbabwe are just as corrupt as . . . ."

or

"I speak three languages and have traveled to twenty-one different countries. Oh, and I can order for us in Italian, Portuguese, or French. What would you like?"

or

"You know, I thought Harvard would be much more challenging. . . ."

or anything along those lines, then Zip It! Even if you are midsentence, just stop. Smile and ask something about him. That way your date doesn't turn into a competitive pissing match. Because ladies, if it does, you lose. Maybe not the argument, but the man.

> **Out-man:** Out-manning happens when a woman strings together a long list of (albeit) amazing accomplishments in the hopes that she will impress a man and he will fall in love with her. News flash: he won't. Out-man a man and he'll give up trying to impress you at all. You've stolen his thunder.

When you try to impress a man, you are stealing his thunder at a time when he might be trying to impress you. So now he feels a little like a lame duck who can do nothing to impress you because you'll always out-accomplish him. He feels like he can't offer you anything. So he figures that he might as well not bother.

If you like him, and you want him to feel man enough to ask you to marry him, focus on learning about him while gently sharing pieces of your own history without bombarding him with the facts. Wait until he asks you the question, like, say, "Where did you go to college?" And even if you went to Harvard, respond humbly. Remember, the smartest of geniuses are the most humble of all. Or if you are a famed geneticist and he asks what you do for a living, you can focus your answer on an entertaining or interesting story about your field. For now, leave out your accomplishments. They aren't what will make him ask you for a commitment. The more time he spends with you, the more he'll discover everything about you—including every single one of your achievements.

If you really want to talk about your accomplishments, you can do so by phrasing them in the following ways:

- "I am passionate about . . ."
- "I'm so lucky that . . ."
- "I've been really fortunate to . . ."
- "It amazes me that . . ."
- "I get so riled up when . . ."
- "Do you know what I find so interesting . . ."

Wrap them around a feeling or an observation rather than just stating it as a fact. This will keep him from thinking of you as an overachiever who may have no time for a man in her life!

And, ladies, beware: If he's a certain type of man (which is more of a boy than a man), telling him about all of your successes might just impress him enough to think, "Maybe she'll take me on her next safari and pay for it!"

Myth #7: "There's a *perfect* man for me somewhere else out there."

Ever heard a woman complain that "he isn't romantic enough" (when she requires a ridiculously specific kind of attention to feel loved), "he doesn't tend to my needs" (when she expects him to read her mind to figure out what her needs are), "he never calls exactly when he says he will" (when she doesn't realize that men have a different sense of timing), and most commonly, "he just doesn't get me!" (when she expects him to fulfill her deepest *unsaid* desires and fantasies)? Seriously, ladies, are these complaints really deal-breakers? Not really. Often a woman will prematurely dismiss a man because of certain qualities or behaviors that she isn't comfortable with because of her own issues (or her crazy checklist that he doesn't adhere to).

So a woman breaks up with an "imperfect man," confident she can find a more perfect one somewhere else. And she does find another man, only to quickly realize that she experiences the exact same problems. Same guy, different name. You know the drill. After a few of those, everything goes to hell in a hand basket. A woman will start to wonder if perhaps the guys are not the problem; maybe *she* is. But the underlying issue doesn't lie where she thinks it does. It's not her appearance or her weight or any other outside factor that's making these men run for the hills. Instead, the issue lies in the fact that she isn't looking simply for a compatible man. She is looking for Mr. Perfect—which, by the way, is a figment of the romantic imagination that is best left to fairytales and *Sex and the City* episodes.

Forget perfect. Perfection is for women who want to stay single. And perfect doesn't guarantee long-lasting love, either. How many "perfect" couples do you know of that have broken up? And even when we say, "they are perfect for each other," what we really mean is that they are quite complementary. You know couples like that—she's super girly and he's a manly man; he's an engineer and she's a free-spirited artist. But what unites them is much stronger than what separates them, no matter how different they seem. They complement each other and she accepts him for his faults and foibles.

Yep, all men have faults and foibles. Man Whispering is not about making him into your perfect man so you can feel "comfortable" thinking you are in control. When it comes to dealing with your man, there will always be something you wish were different about him. And there will always be something he wishes were different about you. Neither one of you is perfect—but you can be perfect for each other if you learn to communicate effectively. That's where Man Whispering comes in and works like a charm. Suddenly the grass will get a whole lot greener on your own side of the fence.

Myth #8: "There's no way Man Whispering will work for immature men."

Yes, it can. Whispering can turn a boy into a mature, masculine man. Why? Because it inspires him to be a man. He is the one solving problems and taking the lead—actions that will naturally steer him to more mature behavior. Whispering allows you to present your wants, desires, and needs in a way that is best understood by the male mind, even when it is still . . . um, maturing. Yes, no matter how immature or selfish your man appears to be, Whispering can encourage him to grow up. Here's why: When you stop taking care of everything, making all the plans and decisions, and doing everything yourself, you give him the time and space to man-up and think of solutions himself. You're also sending the message that you don't accept boyish behavior, whether it be canceling plans at the last minute, being stingy or selfish, or simply acting like a child instead of the man you want him to be. All men love to step in and "take control" of a situation . . . so let him do that and watch him man-up. If you keep doing everything for him and solving every situation, he'll never grow up. And why should he? When laundry "magically" folds itself, why would a man ever think to fold the linens? Typically, men only grow up when we stop taking charge. Appreciate his efforts when he does man-up, and he'll want to do more for you more often.

> **Mature man:** A man who has learned that the world doesn't exist to serve him; instead, he is here to be of service to the world and is generous with his time, affection, and resources.

Myth #9: "Man Whispering only works for men in romantic relationships."

You can whisper to any man in your life—whether it is your boss, your coworker, or your mechanic. If fact, women can whisper all day long. Rather than acting like you have it all together all the time and you don't need anything from anybody, slow down and create the space for men to act chivalrous in your day-to-day life. Certainly, tailor your communication style toward whomever you're talking to—what's appropriate nonverbal communication with your boyfriend isn't appropriate with your boss, for example. But you can use the same principles of requests, observations, and compliments to elicit a positive reaction from any man in your life.

Myth #10: "Man Whispering can change a man overnight!"

There are many things that happen overnight, but changing habits isn't one of them. Be patient with yourself and your man. One of you may slip into old habits once in a while, but keep your eye on the goal. When you slip, learn the lesson and approach the situation differently next time. This new-found communication style is a skill-set that can continually be refined and redefined.

Remember, everyone has the occasional slip—so don't beat yourself (or your man) up over it. Just take some time out to understand your frustrations, and then hop right back onto the whispering saddle.

Myth 11: "My man is going to catch on to my Man Whispering."

He might catch on to the fact that you've become easier to live with and more fun to hang around with. Be pleased by the fact that he actually wants to be around you more often. And even if he does catch on (or catches you with this book in your purse), no big deal. The men we polled love Man Whispering. They crave our appreciation more than we think and deeply want to be the Good Guy. So in their eyes, Man Whispering is a bonus. That's why it's not as if he's catching you doing something terrible to him. Instead you're simply trying to refine your communication style so you two can get on the same page more often. It hurts men when you nag at them. It frustrates and annoys the hell out of them. If Man Whispering can prevent you from nagging your man, trust us: Men say they're all for it.

Remember, men really do want to be better boyfriends, husbands, and lovers. In fact, never before have we seen men grasp a female concept so happily and readily as the men we've polled about this. They instantly gravitate toward it. They support it. They encourage it. They've even given us their two cents' worth to make it easier for us to spread the word. Most important, they've told us that they care deeply about improving communication.

Myth 12: "It's faster if I just do everything myself."

When it comes to many things (but not all!), most women are more efficient than men because we can multitask so well. But, so what? Forget about playing the martyr and doing everything yourself and let him do things once in a while—plan a date, consult on decorating, or cook his favorite meal. You may realize he has some pretty amazing skills you didn't know he had. And most important, you'll show him that you have confidence in him. That's well worth the tradeoff of having to wait a little longer for something to get done.

Man Whispering Mantra
Chapter 2

- Don't get caught up in Man Whispering myths and naysayers. Know your worth and what you want out of your relationship and stick to the principles because they work . . . we guarantee it!

Your Seven-Day Whispering Warm-up

Prepare yourself for Man Whispering success in just one week

"Behind every great man is a woman rolling her eyes."
—JIM CARREY

"Behind every great man is a great Man Whisperer."
—DONNA AND SAM

Look Inward

The beauty of Man Whispering is that it not only brings out the best in your man; it also brings out the best in you. You'll also be more fulfilled, happier, and less stressed than you ever were before.

In order to start enjoying the benefits you'll reap from Man Whispering, you'll need to complete this one-week warm-up. Just as you would stretch out before a run or rehearse a work presentation ahead of time, you need to prepare yourself to Man Whisper. Here's what to do, day by day. It's easier than you think—so let's get the Seven-Day Man Whispering Turnaround started!

Day #1: Gain Perspective

The first step in the warm-up process is to gain some honest and impersonal perspective on your relationship. If anger is currently raging inside you from everything he's done that you're still pissed off about, it's hard to fluff your man's feathers, give him compliments, or get frisky between the sheets. Especially if he forgot your anniversary (or did something else to piss you off) . . . again.

The best way to gain perspective is to get away. Briefly remove yourself from your relationship physically, mentally, and emotionally. That way, you are no longer reactive to all the past triggers and have deactivated your survival "fight or flight" mode. Whether it be a work trip, a night out with the girls, or a quick getaway to your parents', take some time away from your man so you can relax your mind without being on alert to record his next transgression on the relationship scoreboard.

When your mind and spirit are rested, it's easier to come to your senses. This time away is important because it's time to look at who you are, who you want to be, and what you want from your romantic relationship with your man. Make sure in this time away that you commit to being open to trying something new to give your relationship the best chance to be everything you always wanted.

CASE STUDY: THERESA

Theresa, a forty-two-year-old public relations manager, didn't like what her relationship had become. The constant badgering and arguments between her and her husband of twelve years were wearing her down. She felt like she was a drone living in someone else's gray life. When she looked at herself in the mirror, she couldn't believe that the tired face staring back at her was her own. She felt that her husband was always trying to control her instead of giving her love, attention, and support. He wanted to know where she was going, with whom, how her job was, and why she just spent $90 at the hair salon (because she had roots!). So she pushed back, telling him that she could have a private life outside of their marriage. "Stop trying to control my life!" she constantly yelled. Yet her arguments fell on deaf ears, as her husband tuned her out by turning up the TV.

When she went on a vacation to Miami for a friend's birthday, she told her husband that they were going to take a break from speaking for a few days. She wanted to clear her head.

Theresa took her bikini, her sarong, and her favorite cocktail recipe and spent the weekend with the girls by the pool. As the days went on, she felt herself relax. She was having fun chatting with new people and even flirted with the cabana boy. By the end of the weekend Theresa was craving having this sort of fun again . . . but with her husband. And it dawned on her that all his questions were just a way for him to get back into her life—which she had shut him out of by being defensive and irritable. Oops.

On Sunday, her husband called to say he was excited to pick her up from the airport. Time had worked wonders for him as well and he was so looking forward to see her. When she greeted him at the airport, Theresa noticed that her voice was gentler, softer, and more approachable. Instead of being her usual irate, hard-strung self, she realized that a weekend without the usual nagging and tug-of-war proved that their troubles weren't impossible to solve. It also proved that when she was less stressed and in a better state of mind, he was more amenable to listening to what she had to say. And he was happy to please. They both apologized to each other, realizing that they were sweating the small stuff.

When you are in the thick of a tough relationship, it's difficult to get perspective. If you can't manage a weekend away, go for an afternoon of peace and quiet, or even just one hour by yourself. Most often, we need to get away from what we have in order to find the value in it. If you make a habit of doing this once or twice a year, your romantic relationship will benefit from it immensely. For now, use this time away to assess the positive and negative points in your relationship and realize how Man Whispering will make the not-so-good things great, and the good things even better.

Day #2: Forgive Yourself for Your Past Miscommunication Mistakes

We all make mistakes. No matter how stupid yours look in hindsight, it's best to let yourself off the hook. If you don't, it will be extremely tough to be open to learning something new. And most likely you'll find yourself repeating the same communication mistakes that brought you to this place. Recognize that you played your part in the communication problems in your relationship, but then let it go. So many of us think we have to remember our mistakes so we don't repeat them again. But that's not true.

Part of the magic of learning how to whisper to your man is that it changes *your* behavior so you can change your romantic future. It's good to know that just around the corner from every breakdown is a breakthrough. Whispering to men allows you to get straight to the breakthrough by changing the way you communicate with them . . . so you'll have fewer communication breakdowns. And eventually none at all!

> "For three years, I pointed the finger and blamed. And then, I realized, 'Oh my God—it's me too!'"
>
> —SARAH, 36, LAWYER

Let's take a brief trip down your romantic history lane. What went well? What could have gone better? And what part did you play in it? What habits, language, and attitudes did you have in the past that helped create an unhappy relationship? Remember, you're just taking stock, not beating yourself up for anything you did wrong.

Man Whispering Exercise: List the Mistakes You Make When Communicating with Men

Make a list of all the types of behaviors you feel have contributed to a breakdown in your relationships. Be completely 100 percent honest. Do you go out too much, put your needs before his, flirt with your exes, or work all the time? Write it all down.

_____

_____

_____

_____

_____

_____

_____

As you look over your mistakes, you might find yourself justifying some of them. You might be thinking, "But he had just slammed the door to go play pool with his buddies when he promised to stay home with me . . . so I flirted with someone else when I went out that night!" Instead, you might want to ask yourself, "Did I bitch at him when he got home? Did I lay into him the minute he walked in the door? Did I nag and berate him for any reason—even a 'good' one?" If so, you might have contributed to his angry exit.

In relationships, it's always important to recognize your half. If it takes two to tango, then it also takes two to create a mess. You're not exonerating your past boyfriends, either (they made mistakes too)—you're just assessing what *your* role was. It doesn't mean you're letting them off the hook; it just means you're freeing yourself up to move on and not carry around past hurt. By recognizing your part, you allow yourself to be able to change your actions. This, in turn, helps you get a better reaction from your man, which is what Man Whispering is all about!

Day #3: Resolve to Stop Nagging

Today you are going to focus on stopping the nagging, cold turkey—which will, in turn, allow you to create a new blueprint to communicate with your man. Once your man is free from being nagged, he is no longer threatened by you, doesn't become defensive when you ask him questions, and instead of telling you he's a commitmentphobe, will actually want to chase you all the way to the altar. Communicating sans nagging works with your man's natural genetics to create a win-win romantic situation wherein you both get what you want. You will get the Mr. Wonderful he was in the beginning. And he will get a woman whom he feels he can please and provide for.

When you catch yourself starting to nag, using phrases like "Didn't I ask you last week to . . ." or "Why can't you just . . ." or "You should really . . . ," immediately stop. Zip It. Give yourself a Whispering timeout to think about how you can rephrase your requests in a more effective request/observation/compliment format that will bring you better results. Remember, go for using feminine language that makes him want to be the Good Guy.

Nagging is different from lovingly reminding a man to do something. Sometimes he just needs a reminder; we all forget! This isn't a nag. A compliment works wonders, even if its job is to make a request in disguise. For example:

- "Honey, you are usually so good about not leaving your whiskers in the sink. (compliment) Do you think you can keep a better eye out?" (request)
- "You're so reliable when it comes to taking the garbage out on Wednesdays (compliment), I'm wondering what happened today. . . ." (observation)
- "You are so sweet for agreeing to take me to the furniture sale tomorrow. (compliment) I'm so looking forward to it!" (observation)

Day #4: Transform from a Ball Buster into a Woman Worth Climbing a Mountain For

Ball-busting women aren't fun to hang around. A ball buster might think she's doing her man a service by insulting him in the hope that he'll change something, but it only manages to break down the communication barriers. Instead of him trusting and valuing your opinion, he's scared to even be around you for fear that he's done something wrong. Ball busters often find their husbands hanging out with other women—emotionally engaging with the opposite sex in a bid to get a little ego boost without being put down. Ball busters will say, "Can't you just match one darn shirt and tie without my help!?" while a Man Whisperer will tell him how much she usually loves his taste and thinks his choice today is pretty interesting. "But how about this one? You haven't worn it in a while and I think you look hot in it!" Everyone's happy and it's a win-win situation.

On Day #4 of your weeklong warm-up, it's time to accept that you'll need a different approach to dealing with your man: as a softer woman, not a ball buster!

> **Ball buster:** A female who constantly berates and belittles a man, making him feel so emasculated that he gives up trying to please her at all. "Why bother?" he rationalizes. "She's unpleasable."

Instead of bringing a ball buster approach to communicating with your man, you'll need to embrace your inner gutsy babe. A gutsy babe has the insight to know that when it comes to her man, she should focus on being his complement; the yin to his yang.

> **Gutsy babe:** A gutsy babe can still climb mountains, but in romantic relationships she focuses on being a man's complement . . . not his opponent.

Day #5: Learn How to Switch Between Your Alpha Self and Beta Self

There's an Alpha and a Beta babe in every woman. Your Alpha Self is the part of you that is fearless and wants things her way . . . or the highway. To make it in the career world, it's your Alpha Self who climbs the corporate ladder and breaks through the glass ceiling. Don't feel afraid to love your Alpha Self. It's this side of yourself that allows you to do what you want when you want and how you want it. But while that might work for you at the office, your Alpha Self will sink your love life.

The Beta Self of women is just as important. It's your intuitive, more feminine side—the softer side that allows someone else to take care of you. Yes, we know that women can bring home the bacon and fry it up in a pan. But why do it all, when it's much more relaxing and enjoyable to let someone else take care of you and enjoy doing so? Not to mention that by letting your man make decisions and solve problems, you'll find that he develops more confidence and is more likely to please you all on his own.

Whispering is all about learning how to make the switch from your Alpha Self to your Beta Self. First, you want to be aware of when you are tapping into each side. Find and be proud of the attributes of each. Once you identify and balance these aspects within yourself, you can bring out these different aspects at will. For example, if you are up for a raise and your boss asks you how much you want, it's your Alpha Self who asks for what you're worth. And when your man wants to decide which car to buy, it's your Beta Self that kicks in and lets him do the research and figure out the best option.

> **Going Alpha:** When you "go Alpha" on your man, you usurp his power and position as leader. You take away any chance of him thinking that your request was his brilliant idea. "Alpha" is the term used to denote the leader of a pack. Female Alphas are becoming more common as women are kicking ass in the boardroom and taking their newfound powerful attitude into the bedroom. When you "go Alpha" on a man, you are taking control of the romantic situation. Unfortunately, it usually doesn't work. You'll get more if you wait for him to give you what you want rather than demanding it on your timetable.

Some women wrongly think that their Beta Self is weak. Nothing (and we mean nothing!) could be farther from the truth. You know the expression, "You attract more bees with honey than vinegar"? That's what whispering is all about. Women who know how to switch between their Alpha Self and their Beta Self get more of what they want in romantic relationships than do women who are stuck only in one role. (Think of it as similar to being ambidextrous!)

When you are whispering to men, you are tapping into your Beta Self while letting your man play the Alpha role. That's why it's complementary communication. Even at work, you don't have to be all Alpha all the time. A combination of your Alpha Self and Beta Self is a complementary mix—even if you are the boss. Here are some examples of how each Self approaches certain situations:

Alpha Self	Beta Self
Makes the decisions	Enjoys letting a man lead
Wants things her way	Is easily pleased and highly appreciative
Does everything herself	Lets a man take care of her
Must feel in control	Is confident that she'll be taken care of
Is achievement based	Knows she is lovable as she is
Has difficulty receiving from a man	Easily receives from a man
Wants to be equal	Focuses on being complementary
Gives back in equal amounts	Avoids scorekeeping

Part of learning to whisper is to put the goal of improving your romantic relationship above wanting things your way.

CASE STUDY: JESSICA

Jessica is a thirty-four-year-old CEO who wants things her way. She is also known in male circles as a ball buster. Jessica thought she communicated with her boyfriend—they talked every day—but truth be told, he hardly listened to her. Or, if he did, he interpreted it entirely differently from what she intended her words to mean. Jessica ran a *Fortune* 500 company with an iron fist, and she brought the same mentality to her relationship. She wanted her boyfriend to do things her way—pick up his socks when she wanted him to, clean his teabags off the kitchen counter, and get his butt off the couch to lose some weight.

"How many darn times do I have to tell him before he's going to listen?" she complained to us. Therein lies the problem. Nagging treats a man like a child; whispering to him treats him like an adult. We explained to her that the more she demands from her man, the less he hears it. It doesn't matter if you repeat yourself, say it louder, or use every synonym in the English dictionary—men don't register this kind of communication. They defer it, reject it, escape from it, and will eventually run away from it.

We told her to try to whisper to him all the things that she wanted. At first, she resisted: "How will he know exactly what he has to do, then?" she snapped back angrily. "If I don't keep reminding him, he'll never, ever do anything!" But if Jessica continues with her current communication style, she can expect the exact same results: frustrations, exasperation, and despair.

We suggested that Jessica go cold turkey. No scolding, demanding, or telling her man what to do. It means treating him like a man, not like a child or her employee. It also means complimenting him for what he does right; suggesting, at appropriate times (not when the game is on or during sex) what it is she wants him to do; and rewarding him when he actually listens.

After a few days, Mr. Can't-Do-Anything-Right was suddenly morphing into Mr.-Whatever-You-Want-Honey. How? First, Jessica had to make a change in her attitude. She had to learn to bring out her feminine side more often. Next, she used the specific whispering language. At first it felt a little weird and she had to catch herself often, but then came the results. Jessica found that she enjoyed building up her man so much more than bringing him down with nagging. And her boyfriend was responsive, and took action to please her. Of course, their relationship wasn't perfect. But it was immensely better with the new communication style in play.

Jessica committed herself to the good of the relationship and began behaving in ways that was best for it. She channeled her inner gutsy babe (who could jump out of a plane and win any tennis match) into her job. With her man, she learned to soften around the edges in order to let him feel like . . . well, a man!

Day #6: Be Done with Drama

Day six focuses on forgetting all the drama. Sure, we all enjoy a bit of drama. That's why we go to movies, read *People* magazine, and tune in to reality TV. But the dramatic up and downs of romantic strife aren't fun when it's happening to you and your relationship is at stake!

Some of us wouldn't know what to talk about if we couldn't complain about our boyfriends or husbands. But trust us when we say that you're better off singing your man's praises than putting him on the gossip chopping block. Wean your friends off your endless stories of your man's flaws, mistakes, and bad habits. Instead, tell them stories of his generosity, romantic gestures, and commitment!

Day #7: Manage Your Expectations

This is the day to admit that you're human. Hurray for that. Since you're learning, you'll put your foot in your mouth at some point. Just dust yourself off and try again. If you've ever learned how to drive a stick shift, you know that it can be sticky and herky-jerky at first. Once you get the hang of it, you can control the car's performance and speed. But it takes practice! Give yourself and your relationship the time to work out the kinks.

Remember, disagreements are okay. One fight doesn't have to spell the end of your relationship. Sometimes there will be a blowout over who ate all the cookie dough chunks in the ice cream. It's okay. No matter how far off the mark you get, Man Whispering brings you back to a place of complementary balance. Take some time to fume. Then list ten reasons why you are in this relationship and ten reasons why your man is wonderful. Then have a laugh and move on. It's okay to get angry and sometimes feel negative emotions. Just don't stay there or do anything destructive while you're going through them. Channel that energy into something positive—go for a run, take a boxing class, make ten more cold calls, or bake some mean chocolate chip cookies!

Man Whispering Mantras
Chapter 3

- If you find yourself reverting back to your old nagging habits in your romantic relationship, remove yourself from the situation and go back to day one of the program.
- Trust the process and know that the more you Man Whisper, the better your relationship will become.

PART 2

Whispering to the Male Mind

Understand the Male Mind

*The science behind how men
think, act, and love*

*"Women speak because they wish to speak,
whereas a man speaks only when driven to speech
by something outside himself—like, for instance,
he can't find any clean socks."*
—JEAN KERR

*"Don't take men personally. It's not you.
It's just his brain."*
—DONNA AND SAM

We're Not in Kansas Anymore

Ever felt confused about your man's thoughts on commitment or how he shows his true love for you? What about his penchant for porn, beer, and boobs? And why can't he act more like your girlfriends when it comes to talking, sharing feelings, and opening up about his emotions? Welcome to the Male Mind.

It's common to experience crossed wires when it comes to communicating with the man in your life—especially if you think that he has the ability to be (or worse . . . should be) as sensitive to your feelings as your girlfriends are. Rest assured that you're not the only one who's confused; all women have had the same experience. Thankfully, scientists, philosophers, and doctors have come up with an explanation, which points to one body part in particular—and ladies, it's not his penis. It's his brain. By understanding the inner workings of your man's brain and the chemicals it releases in his body, you will better understand why Man Whispering is so effective.

A Man's Brain and Its Hardwiring

We hear it often: Women expect men to behave like intuitive girlfriends who "just know" how you are feeling, always say the right thing, and can tell exactly when it's time for an impromptu cheer-you-up shopping trip and mojito. Unfortunately, most men do not behave like this at all. But it's not their fault; their brain is not set up to think this way. Studies on the brain are incredibly complex and often refute each other's findings. However, we have found similarities in most research that speaks to the common differences between how men and women think, act, and love based on our biological differences.

> "When I catch myself talking to my boyfriend about fashion, hair, or celebrity gossip, I turn it into joke and say, 'Oops. Was I just talking to you about highlights?' and we both have a laugh."
>
> —SANDRA, 28, ACCOUNTANT

This is why you can't expect your man to chatter with you on dates with the skill of a girlfriend, and you can't assume he's not interested in you if he occasionally lets the conversation lapse. Think of it this way: He's simply basking in moments of quiet companionship. If you've ever had a massage where the masseuse just talked and talked and all you wanted to do was zone out—but you didn't want to be impolite but you really wished she'd shut up—well, for men, that describes how they feel being with a woman . . . most of the time.

He Can't Match Your Female-Speak

In everyday life, this means that when you've had a rough day at work or a fight with your BFF, and all you want to do is talk about it (and talk and talk and talk), you can bet your hot handbag that your man is not going to want to hear every nitty-gritty detail again and again. Nor is he going to want to share his emotions with you. Men generally take a systematic approach to data (in this case, life) that doesn't compute emotions, which live outside of time, space, or fixing things. He quite simply just wants to hear the problem (preferably in three words or fewer), come up with a solution (which you may or may not like, but fluff his man feathers anyway for trying), and then to move on to what's for dinner.

This isn't because he doesn't love you—it's just what happens when you are speaking "woman" and he's speaking "man" and you aren't connecting in a way that either of you can understand. Rather, it comes out to him as Swahili. He'll stare at you idly, wondering what the big whoop is and why you're still yammering on. This doesn't mean your problems aren't important to him, or that he doesn't care. It's just that his brain is hardwired to handle different sorts of problems—well, differently.

Unfortunately, this disconnect in communication can go on for hours, days, months, decades, and even whole lifetimes! Two people can live side by side but never actually communicate in a way that helps them to better understand one another; instead, it just gets more confusing than ever over time. Yikes. We've seen it—couples who've been together for decades suddenly facing each other and realizing, "You don't even know me at all!" Unfortunately, that's exactly the trap so many fall into. Fortunately, whispering can pull them out of the abyss—and show them the light.

Don't Expect Him to Remember Much

Ever noticed that no matter how many times you tell your man where the extra rolls of toilet paper are, that you're supposed to go to your mother's house on Friday night for dinner, or where the hamper is for him to put his dirty underwear (rather than the floor), he still can't seem to remember? That's because the part of the brain that forms memories—the hippocampus—is smaller in his male brain than it is in yours, according to research carried out by Simon Baron-Cohen of the University of Cambridge in 2005.

So the next time you find yourself getting mad at having to repeat yourself again and again, take a deep breath. Ask yourself: Is this a big deal? Is it worth sweating over? Or should you just tell him *again* and think about three things he did for you that day—like wake you up with a sweet kiss, and make your lunch for work, and check the air pressure in your tires—that show you he truly does care?

Expect His Sex Drive to Be Vastly Different from Yours

It's no myth that the most powerful sex organ in our bodies is our brain. Since everyone has a brain, you are probably wondering why men are seemingly so much more obsessed with the horizontal hanky-panky than women are. A study reported in *Nature Neuroscience* showed that his male sex drive all comes down to (you guessed it!) the specifics of how his brain operates. Students—both male and female—were given a stack of arousing photographs, and a stack of "neutral" photographs to look at. Scientists then looked at the way both sexes' brains reacted to these images, and they found—surprise, surprise—that a man's brain "lit up" loads more than women's brains when looking at the arousing photographs. Specifically, it was the amygdala and hypothalamus in the male brains that were more activated in the men than in the women. The preoptic area of his hypothalamus, which is the part of the brain that is responsible for controlling his sex drive, is more than two times larger than the same area in your brain. In addition, he has more testosterone running through his veins than you do (causing him to be horny just about all of the time). Combine these factors and it's no wonder the women of the world have a problem on their hands.

So yes, men will want more sex than most women. And they'll want it even after they "forgot" where the hamper is—again. Remember, pick your battles. Forget perfect. Try to remember what he has done for you lately and see if that puts you more in the mood.

He Needs You to Spell Out Your Feelings

Dr. Louann Brizendine, author of the book *The Female Brain*, told CNN that women are better able to empathize with their girlfriends thanks to a woman's "mirror-neuron system." By her reckoning, this system is larger and more active in the female brain, which means, as Dr. Brizendine says, that women can "naturally get in sync with others' emotions by reading facial expressions, interpreting tone of voice, and other nonverbal emotional cues." Men, however . . . cannot. They do not recognize emotions unless they are spelled out for them. Even then, they'll still try to use their brains to solve a problem without bringing emotions into it at all—or recognizing ours. Frustrating for you? Of course. But it's just the way his brain is designed to behave.

So, if you want him to know how you're feeling, spell it out in plain English. Finish this sentence: "Honey, I feel (insert emotion) when you (insert reason why)." Don't expect him to guess or extrapolate from a hint, or he'll be scratching his head for the rest of time. And you'll be standing there with your hands on your hips thinking he's a moron when he's not. Again—remember to focus on creating a complementary relationship. Work within a male brain's capacity by presenting emotional information in simple, easy-to-understand terms.

Men Show It but Don't Say It

Harriet once asked her boyfriend why he rarely told her that he loved her. "What are you talking about?" he replied. "I lent you my car, fixed your computer, and took you out for an amazing dinner last night." Harriet couldn't believe her ears. So this was his declaration of "love"? Was this how men communicated? The story taught Harriet a valuable lesson: If you want to know how a man feels, look at his actions. Men will *show* their emotions rather than *say* them out loud. So instead of throwing a pity party for yourself because he hasn't said anything sweet lately, make a list of all the things he does for you every day for a week. You'll be surprised at how many times he's "showing" you he loves you, even if he's not saying the words.

The Man Trance: Let Him Look!

You know that glazed look men get in their eyes when they see a hot woman? There's a scientific reason for it. According to author, brain expert, and psychiatrist Dr. Scott Haltzman, from an evolutionary point of view, men are designed to want to reproduce continuously over the course of their lives. "It is considered to be in the man's biological interest to get as many women pregnant as possible," he told us during one of our Man Whispering roundtable discussions. "Therefore, men are hardwired to constantly be looking for opportunities to reproduce and for fertile mates." Even if they're married? *Yes*.

We wish we could tell you that there was some magic whispering tactic to trick his brain into thinking that there's no reason to look. We can't. But what we *can* tell you is that his look only lasts a few seconds, and you can focus his attention right back on you by giving him a quick squeeze. His biological makeup and years of evolution are telling him to look at her, but his conscious mind reminds him that you're the one he's with. So don't freak out if he glances at other women now and again.

ALERT! *Porn and Men*

Did you know that 100 percent of men watch porn? In 2009, scientists at the University of Montreal launched a search for men who had never looked at pornography—but they couldn't find any! Therefore, the study concluded that virtually all men watch porn. So ladies, if you find your partner's secret stash, don't get mad. You're going to be hard-put to find a man who doesn't have one.

Man Whispering Mantras
Chapter 4

- Now you know why your man will never be like your best female friend, so quit trying to turn him into one. After all, you *have* great girlfriends—enjoy all the things they're great at doing. Get what you need from them and be fair to your man by not demanding he provide you with the same.
- Remind yourself of how your man is hardwired before snapping at him for not wanting to talk about your mother's sick dog for fifteen minutes.

How to Get the Male Mind to Focus

Why men can't do two things at once (and how you can shift his focus onto you!)

*"I think the larger a woman's breasts are,
the less intelligent the men become."*
—ANITA WISE

"Whispering turns his attention back onto your *breasts!"*
—DONNA AND SAM

Why Men Can Only Do One Thing at a Time

You've probably heard the complaints a million times: "Men can only do one thing at a time!" or, "Men can't multitask!" or worse, "He's not interested in me . . . just the damn TV!" Don't blame the TV, *Playboy* magazine, or his obsession with fixing cars for taking his focus away from you. It's actually his corpus callosum, which sits in his brain. Let us explain. The corpus callosum is the part of the brain that connects the left and the right sides. This section is more developed in a woman's brain, so we can use either side or both simultaneously. Dr. Haltzman tells us that, "when you do a functional MRI, it shows that when you are addressing emotional issues with a woman or using emotional words, both sides of the brain light up, while for men it's either one side or the other." Back in the caveman days, this helped women multitask, while it helped men focus on one thing at a time—which was usually hunting! What many women don't understand is that if you attempt to compete with something your man is already focused on—whether it be work, the television, or fixing his motorbike—you'll lose, every single time. So don't do it. Because not even the character Carrie Bradshaw (who is near and dear to our hearts) could get it right. In fact, we can often hold her up as an example of what *not* to do.

"I could stand in front of the TV naked, bend over, and my husband would ask me to move!"

—DENEE, 27, TEACHER

For example, in the *Sex and the City* episode "The Drought," Carrie puts on sexy lingerie and tries to seduce Mr. Big while he is watching a heated boxing match blaring from the television. She thinks that he will pick sex (and her!) over sports (and beer!). How wrong she was. Mr. Big pushes her away and snaps angrily. Carrie slinks off, takes it personally, and has some serious pout time over it with her girls. Yet Carrie was the cause of her own rejection. Mr. Big didn't deflect her advances because he was being a jerk. Actually, she was the one who was acting like a jerk. Carrie was feeling needy and wanted his attention *now*. She didn't practice patience. She didn't wait to focus his male mind—which was already engaged and focused on the boxing match.

Mr. Big deflected Carrie's advances not because he doesn't love her, and not because he's a loser, but simply because he's a man whose his brain was already focused on another thing.

Five Steps to Shift His Focus

Now that you know *why* men can't do more than one thing at a time, let's figure out how you can cope with this biological fact using Man Whispering. Of course, we have another nice, easy, five-step process for you to follow.

1. Bargain for his time.
2. Wait until you have his focus.
3. Submit ONE request or give him ONE task.

4. Show or tell him the benefits for completing the task.
5. Show appreciation in advance.

Let's look at each step in more detail.

1. Bargain for His Time

Step 1 refers to a clever technique you can use whenever you want to get your man's attention. You're basically giving him a heads-up that a specific event will take place in the future, rather than bringing up something out of the blue when he's in the middle of something else.

> **The Man Zone:** The Man Zone is a man's private mental or physical area where he can let his mind focus on one thing. While in the Man Zone, he prefers to be left alone and will block out any outside interference, including you. If he doesn't actually have a specific "space" or "zone" in which to do this, he will find any hobby or activity to get him out of the house, or set up a space right in the middle of the garage, the garden, or the living room where he can shut off his mind.

For example, tell him you'll accompany him to buy a new set of golf clubs, followed by a delicious lunch at his favorite restaurant—if he doesn't mind if you talk about a topic that's been weighing on you over lunch. That way, you're preparing him for what you're about to say and he can make sure that he has his full concentration on you and the subject at hand during that time. In addition, you're bringing up the issue in-between happy, non-stressful events—like buying golf clubs and eating lunch.

Bargaining for time involves your practicing patience. You don't need everything now—instead, carve out time and request what you want, and then make the time to do it. Practice restraint. You don't have to talk to him *right now* simply because a particular topic is on your mind and you feel that if you don't say something about it immediately, you'll spontaneously combust. Instead, learn to trust the magic of letting him be. Just as a day at the spa does wonders for a woman, so a few hours in his man cave does for a man.

> **Bargain for time:** A Man Whispering tactic to peacefully get your man out of his Man Zone by arranging a time when he can focus on your request. Ask him when it would be best for you to broach a specific topic with him, and then lock him into that time. That way, he'll be mentally and physically prepared to focus all his energy and time on you.

If you absolutely need to communicate what's on your mind every second of every day, try writing it down instead and bringing it up with him later. Having this release for your thoughts may relieve some of your stress so you don't feel the issue is so urgent anymore. (This, of course, is barring a real emergency, in which case you should bust right into the Man Zone.)

CASE STUDY: LILY

Lily was one of those women who just had to say what she was thinking immediately or she thought she would burst. One day, Lily received an e-mail from a guy she had been going out with for three months. It said he couldn't see her this weekend because he had "a guest" in town. "A guest?" she raged. "It's a woman. I know it. I'm going to go out of my mind. I have to find out."

Now, since Lily and her man were still in the early stages of a relationship and they didn't have an exclusive commitment, both he and she were free to do what they wanted with whom they chose to do it—including having an anonymous guest. Demanding to know more about this guest was totally out of line. Instead, she could present the question in a nonchalant Man Whispering way. And that's exactly what she did. She waited (not easy to do!) until he asked her out again and while at dinner, she casually asked him in a light tone with a huge smile, "So, who came to visit you last weekend?" Yes, he dropped his fork, but Lily got her answer. He revealed that he was seeing another woman and that this mystery woman was indeed the anonymous guest. Lily said that's perfectly okay as they don't have a commitment, so he can do what he wants. But she knew she didn't want to play second fiddle to another woman, let alone waste her time with a man who she felt was playing her like a fiddle.

If you're in the same kind of situation as Lily, wait. Practice patience. If need be, write him a nasty e-mail, but save it in your drafts folder. Do not press Send! Wait seventy-two hours and see if you are feeling better. The best-case scenario would be that in a few days you wish him well in a short e-mail. If he asks to see you again, agree to do so. When you meet, inquire about his weekend in a friendly, breezy manner and see what information he offers up. And then go from there. Barraging a man with questions and negative sentiment will only serve to your disadvantage. No man wants to date a crazy psychopath who loses it at any sign of another date being in the picture.

And get this—it could have been a visit from his brother! You just never know. So don't rush into anything.

2. Wait Until You Have His Focus

Even though you've already bargained for his time, you still need to wait till you have his focus. He may be just about to tuck into a succulent steak or is itching for a drink, or is lost and trying to follow a map somewhere. Even though you've scheduled this time to have a talk, it doesn't mean that he's going to be ready instantly. Gently remind him: "Let me know when you're ready to chat," and be patient till you know he's focused solely on you!

Once a man returns from his cave time, he is generally refreshed and is most likely looking forward to connecting with you either mentally, physically, or both! He returns more available and better able to listen because now he's able to focus on you (especially if you didn't badger or call him to ask where he was every five minutes!). Patience and strategy—in the form of understanding where he is coming from when he needs to retreat (not out of anger or dislike of you)—is how you focus the male mind to listen to you, and to be in a space where he willingly is inspired to take action on your observations, requests, and desires.

"This weekend is all about my girl, Erika. She put in a request so I freed it up to give it to her!"

—ARNOLD, 34, ARTIST

Rather than bombard him when he is in his man cave, wait. Again, if you can't wait, try writing down your concerns. And if that doesn't work, then good luck breaking his focus, and get ready to deal with a grumpy guy who isn't listening to you anyway!

3. Submit One Request or Give Him One Task

Now that you have bargained for time and you have his focus, what do you want to focus his one-track mind on? Don't blow it and give him a huge "laundry list" of demands, complaints, or disgruntled comments. Just give him ONE single thing to do or think about. Yes, ONE.

Pick one thing he can do for you right now that would please you the most and request that. Once he's completed it, move on to the next, but don't overwhelm him with too many at once. If you see him starting to freeze up over anything you bring up with him, Zip It instantly and start the process all over again . . . another time. Now, you might be thinking, "This process is glacial." But once your man starts seeing the rewards of pleasing you, he will please you more often. And it'll take him less time to do it because you removed any resistance and procrastination that stems from his fear of being punished. You've also set him up for success by giving him only one thing to do, and scheduling the task at a time he agreed upon.

To satisfy your multitasking mind, it's useful to write down your ten most pressing issues but then tackle them one by one. We know it's hard, but patience pays off. And it pays off big! One well-achieved task, followed by another and another, adds up fast. At first (especially to your beloved Alpha Self), patience will feel as pleasurable as chewing glass. But trust the process. You'll see the glorious results if you do.

4. Show or Tell Him the Benefits for Completing the Task

Another key to focusing the male mind is to let him know that there's a reward waiting for him for a job well done, be it making you smile or the fact that when he does the dishes, it turns you on so much that you jump him and get naked in the kitchen. (Make sure to wait until after he does a good job! After all we don't reward shitty jobs.) Whatever the reward is, create positive associations in his brain that it's a good idea to satisfy your desires. His mind will work like this: "If I do what she suggests, I get sex, my favorite meal, time away, a weekend with the guys, a massage, a happy wife, and more." It's a wise man who knows that "When she's happy, he's happy."

Don't make the mistake of thinking that this process is unromantic. It creates romance! Romance blooms when you are both pleased with each other and getting what you want from the relationship.

5. Show Appreciation in Advance

Even though you want to wait until he completes the task to dole out the reward, thank him in advance for agreeing to do the task in the first place. This is a whispering tactic to set him up for success. It reminds him of all the benefits he'll get once he finds the time to complete your requested task. And the more motivated he is to complete the task, the faster it'll get done. Reminding him of the reward will help speed up the process.

Paying it forward with advance appreciation lets him know that he's on the right track to pleasing you. For men, it's like a flashing neon sign saying, "This way! Over here!" Advance appreciation signals where to go on the road to please you. It also fosters trust in him and in his ability to get it right.

And when he comes up with the solution, remember to let him know that indeed he did get it right. Fluff his man feathers!

Dealing with His Focus on Sex

One question that plagues all women is this: Is he really that focused on sex? Does he really think about having it twenty times per day? And does he really need to relieve himself sexually that many times a week? The answers are yes, yes, and yes. And thank goodness for that. Otherwise, we'd find ourselves begging our men for a little horizontal hanky-panky once a month. And no woman wants that.

Of course, when you're on the first date with a guy, and while you're deciding between the fish or the steak he's just staring at your cleavage and imagining you naked in his bed, it's not the most uplifting experience in the world. But don't punish him for being a man. He's hardwired that way. So you'd better accept it and find a way to love it. . . or you'll find yourself single and alone for life.

Receive His Sexual Energy; Don't Deflect It

The most effective way to manage all his sexual energy is to receive it. Too many women instead deflect their man's sexual energy. They complain that he wants it "all the time" and look at him like some lowly subspecies freak of nature. Sure, he may have a bigger libido than you, and you don't have to do it when you don't want to. However, if you say no to your man, let him know when you will be available for sex. Yes, even with sex you can bargain for time. You can say, "Honey, I'm feeling a lot of stress before this meeting . . . but tonight it'll all be over and I'll be thinking about getting naked all night. How about that?"

This isn't a rejection or a block of energy but a redirection of sexual flow. There are tangible benefits in your request. You negotiated a time when you can both be available and able to concentrate on each other.

Maintaining His Long-Term Focus

So, now that you've learned all about the male mind and its inner workings, you can use this information to your benefit (and his benefit, too!) to whisper to him and keep him focused on things that create harmony and peace in your relationship rather than distance and upset. Whatever you focus on grows. So it's very important to keep your man focused on the positive aspects of your relationship—which could include sex, friendship, love, food, travel—whatever is important to the two of you.

Shape the Way He Thinks of You

Fostering positive associations is key to keeping him engaged and interested in you for the long run. If you are a nag, your man will associate you as his ball and chain and may consider you an ungrateful shrew. At the other extreme, if you provide for him, coddle him, or constantly do things for him that he should be doing himself, he'll associate you with his mother or a sugar momma. But when you let him be the man and graciously receive what he gives to you while guiding him how to please you, you'll be well on your way to relationship bliss.

So you decide. How do you want your man's brain to think of you? Where do you want his focus to be? Are you:

- A bitch who will rip into him if he takes one misstep?
- A mommy who will clean up his messes?

- Or a mentally bright, well-balanced, sexually available woman he would climb mountains for?

Remember, men can only think about one thing at a time. Although we know you have many aspects, just like a multifaceted diamond, he will usually boil things down and create one association for you. That's why you want to take the time to build a good one so that when you do misstep and have an off day, he'll be less reactive, knowing that it's not "you."

We think we know which option you'd choose; after all, you are reading this book! But just in case you picked A or B, we're here to let you know that, unless he's dynamite in the sack and that makes everything else tolerable, it might be time to embrace Man Whispering and avoid those bitch or mommy behaviors. If, however, you picked C, congratulations—you're well on your way to focusing his mind onto you.

Create Memorable Experiences via His Senses

One of the easiest and most enjoyable ways to keep his brain focused on you long-term is to use all five of the senses to create memorable experiences. Dr. Daniel G. Amen, a brain-imaging specialist as well as an author, says that we remember events, people, and places in a negative or positive light based on the brain's associations of the event through the senses.

Pickup artists know this and use it to their advantage. A man practiced in that dubious art can manipulate your brain's associations to get you to feel so safe with him that you invite him upstairs. You, on the other hand, can use this knowledge as a force for good. You can use this information to create positive associations in your man's brain, and do it without manipulation or trying to control him. Here are a few suggestions that show how it's done.

1. **Scent:** Many studies show that different scents activate memories in the brain. So be aware of what scent you are wearing on your body at particular times and what scents you are using when you cook for him. You want the smells to elicit memories of good times at all times. Researchers at Chicago's Smell & Taste Treatment and Research Foundation asked men aged eighteen to sixty-four to sniff thirty different scents. They then measured fluctuations in the men's arousal status as they smelled each scent. The scientists found that orange, vanilla, musk, and lavender got the biggest rise out of the guys. Why? Because they increased the production of alpha brain waves, which made them relax. According to the study's author, Alan R. Hirsch, MD, that relaxation leads to increased arousal. So ladies, start slicing oranges and spritzing vanilla!

2. **Sight:** Showing some skin is the easiest way to get his visual attention. Play up your shape with clothes that complement your figure. Take the plunge and wear a down-to-there-neckline (but make sure you follow the rule that says to wear *either* cleavage or legs—not both!). And forget about wearing the same old comfy yoga pants at home every day. Have fun and dress up for your man, even on a Monday. Men need to be visually stimulated.

> "I used to walk around naked all the time and my husband got so used to seeing me that it was less of a turn-on. Now I wear a silk robe and when I take it off, seeing my naked body makes him want me."
>
> —EVE, 32, PHYSICAL THERAPIST

3. **Taste:** Make sure your cosmetics don't have a chemical taste—especially those permanent lipsticks. Instead, try fruity or vanilla lipgloss that will make him want to lick it off your lips. And we wouldn't recommend letting him kiss your neck right after a spray tan either. When you are sexing it up in the bedroom, make sure everything you want him to touch is washed up, clean, and pleasantly tasty (you know what we mean!). At restaurants, make little bites for him of all the best tasting ingredients in your dish and put a spoonful of heaven in his mouth. He'll love you for it.

4. **Hearing/Sound:** Men will swoon at the sound of your voice saying nice things, and soft music during dinner. You can create special code words that only the two of you know what they really mean.

5. **Touch Him:** Our bodies contain what is called "cellular memory." Your skin actually remembers how you are touched, and by whom. Guaranteed, you touch a man a different way when you are feeling amorous versus when you are feeling angry. Try as much as you can to touch your man only in a way that shows deep affection and feelings of love. This will create positive associations of you in his cellular memory that can last a lifetime. If you've ever heard yourself say, "He makes my skin crawl," it's an example of experiencing cellular memory in a negative way. So make your touch only in a positive light, and with love.

Create Beautiful Memories Together

The better you get at creating positive associations of yourself, the easier you two will be able to create great memories. After all, at every meaningful interaction, you'll be infusing a bit of yourself into the event by appealing to his five senses. To create truly amazing memories together, be ready to put in a little effort.

First do some sleuthing. Find out what he loves to do that he hasn't done in a long time, and then suggest it. For example, if he has a pair of never-been-used motorcycle boots buried deep in his closet, suggest going to the Harley-Davidson store and taking a test drive. Or, dive into his youth. If he used to play guitar, suggest he break it out, blow off the dust, and strum you a few chords. Forget about whether or not he can still play. Let the experience of it be safe, fun, and sexy, and those are the qualities that he will associate with you and the memory itself.

You want his brain to associate you and the memories you create with fun, sex, pleasure, food, peace, adventure, variety, comfort, and all good things. Remember, making great memories is not about perfection. And it's certainly not about control. Keep in mind that men are invigorated by variety. Changing your routine and being spontaneous socially and sexually re-sparks his brain and zest for life. When his brain associates positive memories with you, he'll stay because doing so is worth it.

Here are some other ways to create Man Whisperer–caliber memories:

1. Do something with your partner that is a little dangerous and on the edge, like riding a roller coaster, skydiving, or rock climbing. The adrenaline will make your blood flow and your heart pound quicker. You'll cling to your man like he's your savior, and your bond will instantly strengthen. And the experience will be something that you two will remember together for a long time to come!

2. If you're in the early stages of your relationship, go away on a romantic trip together for two to four days. It's the perfect way to test the waters, create memories together,

and experience the new spark of your relationship. (But Man Whisperer it when you suggest it!) Go hiking, biking, skiing, or do something energetic and outdoorsy. You'll release endorphins and by the end of it, you'll be making googly eyes at one another and plans to go on a lot more vacations!

3. If you're living together, don't forget the power of the "date night"—but drop the routine of it and go for variety. For example, get dressed separately (you in something new—or even better, something you wouldn't usually wear!) and meet each other at the restaurant. Make it sexy and fun, and bring back the memories of the two of you together from when you first started dating. Do this at least once a month (if not more) and you'll have your man looking at you with lustful eyes even at those times when you're sporting pimple cream, unsightly hair growth, and a very not-sexy shower cap.

4. If you're already married, combine all of these methods. Do something dangerous every so often; plan trips together; schedule regular sexy, fun, and varied date nights; and leave the kids at home with a sitter or with a family member. Rent a lovely hotel room if you can, even if it's in your hometown. Get your hair done for the occasion, buy a new dress (or wear his favorite one), and indulge!

Once you've embedded these great memories, use triggers to remind him of the positive associations. For example, if you went on a dream trip to Italy and you two always talk about that special restaurant in Florence, re-create the night by surprising him with the sights, sounds, and smells of Italy. Or put on the dress you wore on your first date. A dash of "sex" perfume can signal him to run into the bedroom.

Man Whispering Mantras
Chapter 5

- Bargain for time to find a mutually agreeable point to discuss issues.
- Make just one request or give him only one single task at a time, and reward him for his efforts.
- Get your man to pay more attention to you over the long term by creating exciting experiences and lasting memories together.
- Let him make positive associations with you via your five senses.

Commitment and the Male Mind

Conquer his "Anti-Commitment Gene"
(to make him want you forever)

"Women might be able to fake orgasms. But men can fake whole relationships."
—SHARON STONE

"Man Whispering will get your guy to commit, for real!"
—DONNA AND SAM

The Biology Behind His Action

The fact that men want to have sex with as many women as physically possible is not only a biological fact, but is also a cliché that most women would rather not hear. But here's the catch: Women are genetically wired to want men to stick around to protect and provide for their babies.

Physically, men aren't as invested in what happens after sex as women are. Men have millions of sperm to burn versus our one or two eggs per month. That's why it's best for women to be way pickier than men when it comes to mating. Yet it's not a man's fault that he is genetically wired to have sex with as many women as he can. It's not a weakness. There's no sense being angry at biology. Instead, learn how to work with it—go with its flow—and use this hot tidbit of information to your advantage.

So how do you go about doing this? Get whispering! The sooner you learn how to get your man to think that monogamy is actually a good idea, the sooner he'll stop just having fun and want to commit to you for the long run. Certainly, some men decide on their own at some point that they're tired of casual sex. These men discover that one day, their thoughts have shifted from sex, porn, and beer to wanting to build a family and create a meaningful life with (gasp!) one woman. Suddenly their hearts yearn for something more like little baby toes to squeeze and a smiling wife to wake up to every morning. As Miranda Hobbs from *Sex and the City* once said, "Men are like cabs. When they're available, their light goes on." The light she describes is what turns on when a man decides that he's ready to "settle down" and start a family. The boy is ready to become a man and not think only about himself (and his sexual body parts) anymore.

ALERT! *What Do You Really Want?*

Decide if you're really into *him* or if you're just into the *idea* of him. Do you spend more time fantasizing about something (marriage, kids) than you do actually spending real quality time getting to know him? The authors of *The Myth of Monogamy*, David P. Barash, PhD, and Judith Eve Lipton, wisely point out that it is indeed a challenge to live in a monogamous society when men's brains are wired to be polygamous. What helps create a middle ground is to let men know just how worthwhile commitment is and what's in it for them. Otherwise, men will continue to run from commitment and continue to be Mr. Fun Guy forever.

Truth be told, even those dreamboat men admit that monogamy is tough. Sometimes, *really* tough. Their biological makeup makes them still want to sleep with other women . . . but they don't. Why? Because a man like this values the woman he is with more than the temporary thrill of a new conquest. He knows that he risks his wife or girlfriend leaving him if he ever so much as entertains the thought of straying. And he knows he has it good because she whispers to him just how good it can be. He doesn't want to risk losing her and the wonderful life that comes with her.

The Man Whisperer Secret: Show Him Why Monogamy Is Good

So what makes a man ready for commitment? And conversely, what makes other men out there tout the mantra "fifty is the new twenty" and resist commitment to the bitter end, when they're down to the last hair on their balding heads? It's all about timing and understanding the primal biological urge that males have to mate as often as they can with as many women as they can and not feel like a "bad guy."

True, boys don't become men overnight, but whispering certainly accelerates the process. Therefore, it's up to you to show men the benefits of monogamy and just how delicious and wonderful it can be. Every man fears marrying his princess only to later wake up to a chronically displeased shrew for the rest of his life. Knowing that this is his top fear gets you halfway to commitment. Through whispering, you can allay all his commitment fears one by one until he has no fears left. When you whisper to a man about the benefits of being with you every day, he'll stay because he knows that he'll get more of what he wants from life by being committed to you rather than by remaining single.

> "What's the big deal about sex? We should all just be having fun!"
> —DANNY, 27, ASPIRING PICKUP ARTIST

Let's be honest. Fun is . . . well, fun! And monogamous relationships are famed for being tough—even at the best of times. No one is quoted as saying that marriage is easy. Whether you like it or not, it's up to you to redefine for your man that commitment isn't a ball-and-chain kind of deal, but one that allows a couple to build a life together and develop as individuals. Too many women think that once they have "The Ring," they own their man and he is under their thumb and must submit to their demands. *Au contraire!* That type of behavior is one of the predominant reasons why men protest and resist monogamy and are reluctant to commit.

Commitment's Archenemy: Casual Sex

Another major reason why men are so darn reluctant to commit is the lure of casual sex. Today, women are making it easier than ever for men to get into their pants. And it's screwing things up. Why? Because it actually encourages a man's Anti-Commitment Gene, rather than talk it down. In earlier generations, folks got married so they could have sex. Today, that may sound ridiculous at best—but one thing it did was make men commit. With modern women taking the Pill and having casual sex like men, men have just about zero reason to commit to a woman.

ALERT! *His Anti-Commitment Gene*
The physical genetic wiring that programs men to have sex with as many women as they can. For a man to go against his genetic wiring, you must whisper to him something he wants even more.

It's hard for men to put any value on something they achieve so easily—which includes getting into any woman's pants, including yours! So if your man isn't giving you the level of commitment that you want, ask yourself, "What is he getting for free?" Know what you are just giving away, then put a value on it. If you don't, he never will.

How to Get a Man to Commit: Phase 1

Once you've begun addressing his ongoing fears, you can make real headway in getting your man to commit. When you use the following steps to get a man to commit (no matter how long you've been with him), you don't need to be afraid of a man's Anti-Commitment Gene. It doesn't rule your love life. You aren't victim to it! Instead, you will know that he is going to chase you until he pins you down because he believes that you're worth sacrificing casual sex for. What he has with you is worth way more than chasing other women. You can have men eating out of the palm of your hand, chasing you, doting on you, and being desperate to pin you down as soon as possible. Here are the five steps:

1. Know what level of commitment you desire from a man. Ask yourself: What kind of relationship are you ready for in life? A boyfriend, marriage, kids, a casual lover? What stage are you at in your life? What do you want? It's only when you know what you want that you can match it up to see if he is available to offer it to you.

2. Be the type of woman he feels safe committing to. Men don't want to commit to women whom they think will make their greatest fears come true. And they also don't want to commit to women who are too easy. Why?

Because men commit by providing for us; they commit with their money. A man needs to know you are trustworthy and worth his saying no to all the other women in the world. It's important for you to know what makes you worth the price of commitment. That is part of knowing your worth!

> "I've been happily married for nineteen years. But that also meant I had to become a morning person. My husband is at his best before 10 A.M. While we were still dating, I started waking up early to enjoy that time with him. It's been worth every minute and a very small price to pay."
>
> —LAUREL, 41, PUBLICIST

3. Whisper to him all the reasons why it's a good idea to go against his biology and commit to you. (See the following section, Allaying a Man's Fears of Commitment.)
4. Say no to everything that isn't what you want in a relationship. If you're ready for marriage, you need to stop dating playboys (and boytoys!) who just want to play around. Instead, start acting like marriage material. If you're in a committed relationship and you're ready for kids but he's all about sex, drugs, and rock 'n' roll—well, that's an incongruity you need to rectify before you start a family.
5. Wait and be patient!

Allaying a Man's Fears of Commitment

A good Man Whisperer finds out what her man's greatest fears of commitment are, and then whispers the opposite to him. For example, if he fears that he'll never go on another guys' trip again, say, "It's so cool how Jeff and Sarah take separate vacations every once in a while. It's good to trust each other to have some time alone!" Here are some other common fears men have and how you can counter them with Man Whispering:

- **He'll never get any peace and quiet.**
  Whisper: "Sometimes, I just love not talking. Peace and quiet is so relaxing."
- **You'll spend all his money and make him go broke.**
  Whisper: "I just don't understand how women can be so ridiculous with money. I love budgets. It lets me know how much I have to spend."
- **You'll never be happy.**
  Whisper: "Just being with you puts a smile on my face!"
- **He'll be your slave.**
  Whisper: "Honey, you haven't gone (insert favorite activity) in a while—why don't you call up your buddies and head out?"
- **He'll be stuck with a fat, bitchy wife.**
  Whisper: "Exercise is super-important to me. I plan on being in shape my whole life."
- **He'll never get to burp, fart, or watch porn again.**
  Whisper: "Oops, was that a fart? Let me open a window."

How to Get a Man to Commit: Phase 2

If you've been working on the previous steps for months and he still hasn't committed, it's time to take things to the next level. At that point, use these three steps:

1. Give yourself an Inner Ultimatum (more on this next).
2. Focus on yourself and what you will do if he chooses not to commit.
3. If nothing else has worked, it's time to have the dreaded "Talk" with him—Man Whisperer style!

Let's look closer at the parts of this three-step plan.

Using the Man Whispering Inner Ultimatum

So many of us find ourselves waiting, waiting, and waiting for a man's light to come on. This is the month, you may think. Or this will be the anniversary when you see a sparkling ring. Or, if you already have the ring of your dreams, you think *this* will be the month that he remembers a little bit of romance goes the distance. Even if you've been together months or years and there's still no sign of the level of commitment that you want, whispering to him can make your dreams come true.

ALERT! *It's Not a Commitment Unless He Says It Is*

If it's a commitment that you're after, keep this in mind: Your relationship might look and feel like commitment, but until he asks you for one, you don't have it.

Luckily, there is a way to whisper to his Anti-Commitment Gene without saying a word. And it works wonders! We call it the "Inner Ultimatum." Simply decide what you want (in other words, your requirements for staying in the relationship) . . . in your mind. Tell yourself that if you don't get what you want within a certain amount of time, you are prepared to walk away. (Of course, if he doesn't make his deadline—you can let him in on your Inner Ultimatum as a last resort before you go . . . but most often you don't have to!)

> **The Inner Ultimatum:** A silent agreement with yourself about how much time you're willing to give and what you let a man get from you mentally, socially, spiritually, and sexually without the commitment you want. If he exceeds his time limit or wants more than you are willing to give, let him go. There are millions more fish in the sea.

Drawing the line in the sand (in your own mind!) is a powerful thing. This technique works because men have a sixth sense about when a woman is at the end of her rope and is ready to leave. But by setting your own deadlines privately and prematurely (before you are *really* ready to leave!), you can accelerate what you want in your relationships. Know and be firm about what you will and will not give to a man without the level of commitment that you want. Once you decide on your Inner Ultimatum, stick to it! Don't stay in a relationship you don't feel right about . . . not even if the sex is mind-blowing. No amount of good sex is ever worth staying in a relationship you don't feel cherished in.

Too often we've seen women compromise on their requirements to be with a man, but in doing so they only hurt themselves. For example, you'll move in when you aren't ready, act like a couple when he hasn't yet referred to you as his girlfriend, or let him talk to you on the phone for hours without asking you out. Anytime you break a promise to yourself for a man's company, you are making a decision out of fear—not self-confidence. Instead, you need to think that if he isn't the one, you'll find another man who will be available to give you what your heart desires. When a man wastes your time, it's because you let him waste it . . . so don't blame him. Instead, draw the line in the sand that gets you what you want for yourself in a relationship.

Focus on Yourself

Some women become so focused on having a man in their lives that they forget that their own lives existed before the relationship. If you find yourself in commitment limbo, shift your focus back onto *your* dreams and goals. If you've always wanted your master's degree, start investigating what school you'll like to attend. Or start planning vacations you've always wanted to take. Simply put, start imagining a future for yourself that looks bright. That way, if that unfortunate situation occurs and you don't get a commitment, you are not blindsided. You'll already have begun to lay the groundwork for moving on.

Your Last Resort: The Dreaded "Talk"

No matter how long you've been with your man, when you aren't getting the level of commitment you want from him, you sometimes must resort to "The Talk." Unfortunately, if done incorrectly (which it is most of the time), it can have disastrous results; the man in question feels cornered and most likely will try to flee from what he sees as the "pressure"! You may then be prone to bitch and complain to your friends (which contradicts Man Whispering Mantra #7) about how a real man wouldn't have been afraid to commit. But rather than putting the little boy in him in a corner and demanding things that he isn't ready to give, it's better to whisper to the part of him that is a man.

The Initial Talk

If you really, really want to know where you stand in your relationship with your man (and yes, you certainly are entitled to this information!), remember that demanding to know something immediately threatens him. It makes him feel trapped and instantly puts him into his "fight or flight" mode. Instead, set up boundaries inside your head. Then whisper them to him. Ask him when a good time would be to talk about your relationship. At the agreed-upon time and place (be sure it's not in your bed before or after sex), begin the discussion by telling him that you understand that he might not know all the answers to your questions up-front. Casually drop into the conversation that you're really enjoying hanging out or that you're "into" the relationship, but you're feeling that this is a time to chat about what he wants in a woman and if he sees himself committing to you. Don't tell him that commitment is what you want. Instead, phrase the question this way: "What is the type of relationship you are able to commit to?"

> "My biggest peeve is when women ask me way too soon where this is going. I don't know. I'm still getting to know her."
>
> —GREG, 35, SALES MANAGER

Then ZIP IT! Let him deal with it. Give him some peace and quiet to mull it over, and then listen to what he says to find out if it matches up to what you want. Ask him when would be a good time to talk about it again. Give him the time, space, and peace and quiet to work it out. Remember, you're trying to communicate the benefits of committing to you while simultaneously being true to yourself.

The Waiting Period

In the meantime, subtly bring your attention back to yourself as you wait for his answers. Start mentally preparing to meet other men. Get a manicure and get your hair done. Go out more often with friends, and don't ask him to join you. Become more independent and less predictable. Focusing on yourself will spur your man into action. He'll begin to miss you. He'll begin to wonder if there are other men out there pursuing you. He'll begin to think that if he doesn't pin you down, some other man will, and he's going to miss out on the woman of his dreams. Thus, he comes to his decision to commit all on his own—but his decision is based on your actions. This process takes courage. It takes strength and discipline. But you're worth it. And he's got to see that for himself before he can decide to give you what you want in order to continue the relationship.

Whatever you do, *don't cling*. Clinging can have two very different outcomes, neither of them good. It either will create an intense attraction that makes him *have* to come to you rather than *want* to—or, worse, it will push him away because it plays into his fears that he'll be smothered if he does commit to you!

More often than not, before your Inner Ultimatum timeline is up, you'll have what you want. Mission accomplished!

The Follow-Up Talk

If, on the other hand, his time is up and your man hasn't muttered a word about commitment or where you two stand, let alone tried to make plans with you for the following weekend, give him one more shot by explicitly telling him your Inner Ultimatum.

Tell him exactly what you require to allow him to continue seeing you. "I'm really excited for our future and value what it's going to bring us, so I'm giving this a couple more days/weeks/months to see what happens." Then Zip It. See what he does. If it's nothing, then move right along. Clearly, this won't be easy—but the good news is that you're already primed to meet another guy, as you've already become more independent. Remember, no man is the last man on the planet. You are way too fabulous to waste your precious time (your time *is* precious!) and energy on a man who is unable to give you what you want.

Beware the Faux Commitment

Until you both agree that you are in a committed relationship and you are on the same page about what that means, you're not. We don't care what time with him looks like, tastes like, or smells like. Men can act as if they are committed to you for the rest of eternity but, in reality, they are playing the field. They might even pretend to make plans for the future. They may tell you again and again all the things they like about you. They might even mention the "L" Word. "I love a girl who eats meat," they'll say when you take a bite of your burger. They might even make plans for the future, like "Would you prefer to go to Paris in the spring or the fall?" But unfortunately, as you will learn in the next chapter, men will do and say just about anything to get into your pants. Including dropping an "L" Word or two into the conversation knowing that you'll put more meaning on it that it has.

> "I try to sleep with every girl I'm interested in right away. If she resists my advances—and actually sticks to it!—then I know she's different."
>
> —JAKE, 26, MARKETING EXECUTIVE

Until men verbally agree to a commitment to you, you aren't in a committed, monogamous relationship, no matter how good it feels to be with him. And if after six months of Faux Commitment (even if it seems like the real deal since you're hanging out with him all the time!), if you bring it up, be prepared for him to run away, saying, "I thought we were just having fun!" In that case, don't worry if the door hits him on his way out. And there's no need to be angry, either. Remember, men by nature want to have fun for as long as they can. Which means they will string us along . . . for as long we let them. This is why your Inner Ultimatum is so important. It draws the line in the sand as to what you require from your man in order to spend your precious time with him.

CASE STUDY: SUSAN AND KEN

Susan had been in what seemed like a steady four-month relationship with a man she thought was a super-catch. He was handsome, successful, and very generous. Ken was consistently asking her out two or three times a week. They did couple-y things together like going shopping for couches for his apartment, seeing French films, and taking long beach walks on the weekends. And Ken always called Susan (no texting!) to arrange dates. Susan knew in her heart she was ready for a committed romantic relationship that was marriage-bound. And because everything seemed like a commitment with Ken, she had stopped seeing other men.

But Ken still hadn't asked for a commitment. Susan didn't want to scare him away by having The Talk, but she was starting to wonder if indeed they did have something more than just a good time together. She certainly didn't want to waste a year only to find out he was just having fun.

To put the ball back in her court, first Susan needed to flip her point of view. She needed to realize that Ken wasn't dangling the keys to her heart . . . she was! And if Susan was going to give him the key to her heart, Ken had better do something to make her feel safe doing it. Instead of working herself up into a tizzy and wasting her time complaining to anyone who would listen, Susan kept busy, beautiful, and positive. Ken soon noticed the shift in her personality. He began to want to be more of a part of her life. He began inquiring about her days more often, and asking her out for dinner a few days before the day he wanted to see her. Lo and behold, he mentioned his brother's wedding one night over dinner, and asked her to be his date.

"As what?" she replied halfheartedly. "Your stylist?"

"As my . . . girlfriend," he said, smiling back.

"Are you asking me for a commitment?" she asked.

"Yes," Ken smiled, because commitment was his idea.

Susan couldn't wait to see how Ken acted around his family and how they treated one another. She knew it would clearly cement whether he was the type of man she could see herself settling down with, or not.

This is a prime example of how you can whisper a Faux Commitment into a real one. If you find yourself in a full-on Faux Commitment, the solution is to start dating other men. Of course, it may feel at first like chewing glass—after all, you want to be with him—but if he isn't giving you what you want, you have to move on. This way, you'll be available for a man who *is* able to commit to you, rather than be wrapped up in someone who will string you along for as little as he can for as long as you are willing to put up with it. The bottom line is that a man is only able to commit to a woman who is first committed to her own well-being. Be busy, be active, be lighthearted, be fun, be easygoing, and be willing to go easy on yourself.

108 · The MAN *Whisperer*

Man Whispering Mantras
Chapter 6

- It's a fact of life that most men want to sow their wild oats. And it's your timing and your actions, including drawing the line in the sand, that will make him want to stop screwing around, settle down, and commit— to you.
- Give yourself an Inner Ultimatum about what you want and when you want it. If you don't get what you want, you walk. Stick to it!
- If your man doesn't commit to you in due course, remind yourself that there are hundreds of other men out there who would gladly fill that position. Don't get stuck on one dude just because he's playing hard to get. You're better than that!

PART 3

Whispering to Capture His Heart

CHAPTER 7

The L-Word

Get him to say " I love you "
(without it freaking him out)

"If somebody says 'I love you,' to me, I feel as though I had a pistol pointed at my head. What can anybody reply under such conditions but that which the pistol-holder requires? 'I love you, too.'"
—KURT VONNEGUT, JR.

"Whispering inspires men to say 'I love you' first and think it was their brilliant idea."
—DONNA AND SAM

Waiting for Those Precious Words

Are you at the point when feelings of love are rushing through your veins faster than you ever imagined? Do you desperately want to say "I love you" to the man who makes you feel like angels are singing in your heart? But maybe you feel that if you wait for him to say it first, those three little words will be a whole lot sweeter. Well, you're absolutely right.

Of course, the sheer suspense (and desperation) of it all is killing you! The desire to express your love for him is building up in you like a pressure cooker ready to explode. Every day that passes, you want to say it even more and it's getting harder and harder to bite your tongue.

So what's a gal to do?

Zip It, that's what.

The Case for Zipping It

Why should you Zip It? Because it is so much sweeter when making the next move in your relationship is his brilliant idea. And the majority of men we've polled feel exactly the same way. Forget how to lose a guy in ten days; if you want him to imitate *The Scream* painting, just say the "L" word before he decides he's ready, and he'll be out the door faster than a speeding bullet.

When you put a man under the hot, burning "So . . . do you love me too?" spotlight, he'll have as much desire to utter those three words as he does to go handbag shopping with you on a sale day. That'll be his reaction if he hears the word "love" prematurely. And prematurely is exactly when so many women are inclined to say it. It's not entirely our fault. As we've explained, women are biologically predisposed to bond to men faster than men will bond to them.

So, what now? Man Whisper, of course!

Remember, Man Whispering doesn't force a guy to do anything. Instead, it leverages the fact that most men (who aren't boys or players!) want to please you. And if you whisper correctly, he'll know that one of the things that will make you deliriously happy—when the time is right for him—is to declare his love for you.

Of course you might be thinking, *Isn't this the twenty-first century? Why can't I tell a man I love him? Why can't I make an executive decision (like I do at work all day long) that it's okay for a woman to say "I love you" first?* Sure, you can go right ahead say, "I love you" before he even fathoms mentioning it to you. But, you'll also put the brakes on him chasing you. We can smell the burned rubber right now.

If you really want to Man Whisperer to his Anti-Commitment Gene, your timing is critical. Wait for it! Trust us when we say we've seen too many cases of premature "I love you" scenarios gone wrong. That's why we don't recommend saying it before a man does, ever. We've heard too many women risk it all and tell their men, "I love you," only to be offered in return an embarrassing "thank you," "Wow, isn't it all a bit too soon?" or worse—"I though we were just having fun." Yeouch.

> ## ALERT! *Avoid Backing Him into the "I Love You" Corner*
> Telling a man "I love you" first instantly puts him into a pressure cooker. He doesn't see this as a sweet, kind gesture, but one of impatience and coercion. He instantly feels that you are making an invisible demand on him to say it back. He fears that maybe it's all too soon and that by saying it back to you, he's leading you on or locking himself into a commitment he isn't ready for.

Of course, you'll hear the one-in-a-million story of a woman who said "I love you" first and everything worked out. Lucky her, you might think. But trust us, she was the exception to the rule. Remember, if you want to win, it's wise to play by the rules—not the exception.

The "Sex = Love" Theory: Why Women Confuse Love with Sex

As you now know, when it comes to men, love, and sex, they're just not hardwired like you. As Billy Crystal once said, "Women need a reason to have sex. Men just need a place." The truth is that women are more emotionally susceptible in the aftermath of sex than men are. When you sleep with a man, you release a hormone called oxytocin, also known by scientists as the "cuddle hormone."

According to researchers at the University of California, San Francisco, the more often you have sex with a man, the more emotionally bonded to him you become because of the oxytocin you release. It doesn't matter if it was good sex or it left you saying, "That was it?" And it doesn't matter if you just met him. You're bonded, baby! Oxytocin is the "love drug," and your body likes it and immediately wants more of it. Your mind tricks you into believing that it's all because you're in love with the guy who's activating all these surging hormones.

"Must get more oxytocin!" your body robotically signals your brain. Your body doesn't care if you have to have sex with Mr. Wrong or Mr. Player to get it. You can be instantly addicted to it (not to him, mind you . . . but to the oxytocin rush you get from him) and you're hooked. Your body just wants more, more, and more! That's why it can be so hard to break up with a guy even though you know (and everybody else knows!) he isn't right for you; your body is chemically bonded to his. You may think it's love, lust, or a thousand other things, but the truth is that you're addicted to the oxytocin released when you have sex with him, see him, smell him, or listen to his voice on his voice mail twenty times.

Once you're bonded, you have to take control of your body's oxytocin urges, as much as you have to overpower a broken shopping cart that veers too much in one direction. When your body starts pulling you in his direction, you need to interrupt the urge and think, "No!" Before you call him at one in the morning, stop and ask yourself, "Is it me . . . or is it the oxytocin talking?" Don't do it. Wait. At least seventy-two hours, to be exact.

The Seventy-Two-Hour Rule

When you are considering blurting out "I love you" first, remember the Seventy-Two-Hour Rule: It can take seventy-two hours for your body to be cleared of an addictive substance (and to be on the other side of withdrawal symptoms). So right after you have a burning desire to get closer to him when you know it isn't good for you, wait three whole days before you contact him. (That means no stalking him on Facebook either!) Self-control is the only way to completely detox yourself off him. You will no longer be under the influence of your hormones, so you can make a more rational decision. Your mind will be stronger than the oxytocin pumping through your veins. Outsmart the hormone by saying "No!" to your oxytocin-induced impulses.

> **The Seventy-Two Hour Rule:** To see if it's the oxytocin talking (or any other hormonal urge or surge), wait seventy-two hours and see if you still feel the roaring desire to tell him that you love him or any other confession about to roll off the tip of your tongue.

"Will He *Ever* Say It?"

As you can tell, women are much more likely to say "I love you" than men are. If you want him to speed up the process, start whispering. That way, you inspire him to say it—rather than making a "Say you love me or else" demand. First, he needs to know that you won't go crazy on him (as some women do) thinking that now he's yours, you own him and you are allowed to suddenly become clingy, needy, and demanding. Your man needs to know that even if he is committed to you and says "I love you," he is still (relatively) free.

ALERT! *How Some Men Use the "L" Word to Get Sex!*

Some men will date you for a nanosecond and then tell you that they love you. Sure, we all want to believe that true love can really happen that fast. And of course, you deserve it. But unfortunately, some men are manipulators. They have learned the power of a simple "I love you" and its ability to get women in bed faster than if he said his name was George Clooney. Science backs up this theory. According to a study carried out by Southeastern University, significantly more men than women will say "I love you" sooner than they mean it for one reason only: sex. Yes, ladies, these three words aren't sacred to everybody. Certain men will lie to get you in bed. Why? Because men are biologically programmed to deposit their sperm into as many women as possible. And some men cleverly (and maliciously) will use the I-Love-You script to do so. If his "I love you" seems too soon to be true, it probably is.

Remember, whispering is not about manipulating the wrong guy into thinking he loves you; it's about getting the *right* guy in your life to acknowledge his feelings for you when he's ready. You're just nudging him ever so slightly out of his set man-ways into someone who isn't afraid to express his love.

CASE STUDY: AMY

After waiting nine months for the "I love you" declaration, Amy, a thirty-nine-year-old actress, was fed up. "What the hell is wrong with him?" she asked us. After all, she was successful, gorgeous, and talented. She couldn't quite understand why he just wouldn't utter the words. More to the point, what type of desperate vibes was she putting out there that made him so nervous to say it?

We encouraged her to exit the situation in order to reactivate his "Pursue Gene." And so she booked a two-week trip to visit family in London. She turned off her phone and refused to check her e-mail. She Zipped It on that subject matter and let him "fix it" without demanding a thing.

Lo and behold, when she turned on her phone a few days later, there was a text message from her boyfriend with these three simple words: "I miss you." Close. But not yet. She then texted back, "Why do you miss me?" A few hours later, she saw the words she'd been waiting for: "Because I love you. Come home soon." She couldn't believe what she was reading!

Removing yourself from the situation has a magical ability to bring out the "L" Word in a man. This is because in becoming slightly unavailable, you reactivate his Pursue Gene, which keeps him interested. This strategy works every time, because it causes dopamine and testosterone to surge through a man's veins. Your absence creates a space in which he realizes that he needs to take action to deepen the relationship rather than risk losing you.

Why Do You Need Him to Say "I Love You" So Badly, Anyway?

Once you think you need something, you give your power away. The truth is you don't actually need him to say "I love you." Sure, you may *want* him to. But you won't die if he doesn't. It's just a chemical spell your body is under—especially if you slept with him without a commitment! Your mind and heart want to catch up with the physical commitment your body made and equalize the situation.

Instead of needing him to say "I love you," think to yourself, "I'm lovable. If he loves me, he'll say it when he's ready to. And if he doesn't, I'll be able to handle the situation and find a solution."

But . . . if you absolutely can't wait for him to say it, you can soften by the blow by making a comment or an observation instead of putting him in the "I love you" corner.

If you feel you simply must bring up the "L" Word in conversation, we advise you to use the following questions, which are relatively gentle:

- "Are we in love?"
- "Is this love?"
- "When do you think is the right time to say 'I love you'?"
- "How do you know when you are in love with someone?"

Whatever variation you use, don't make it a yes-or-no answer. You are asking his expertise on the love question and letting him solve it, fix it, and show off just how much he knows about love and relationships. And remember, some men fancy themselves to be Mr. Romantic. Just as a man may dream of one day proposing to the right woman, he may also dream of one day saying "I love you" . . . to you.

Five Whispering Steps to "I Love You"

Now that you know the basic premise of how to whisper so a man will say those three little words, here's the five-step plan in more detail:

1. Don't demand that he say it.
2. Make him feel safe if you ever want him to say it.
3. Be the woman he wants to say it to.
4. Remove yourself from the situation if you feel he's the one but you're being too needy or available.
5. Zip It and practice patience.

Let's talk about each of these steps in depth so you get the full picture.

1. Don't Demand It

The key to whispering to his heart is speaking in a language he understands. When you say "I love you" first, it's akin to giving him a command or demand, even if it doesn't appear that way to you. Your initiative makes him think that you expect a certain reciprocal response from him. And if his response isn't what you were hoping for, he knows that here come the tears, the fight, the drama, and the trouble.

Demanding anything is in strict violation of Man Whispering Mantra #10. He'll instantly feel pressured to say it back, which triggers the "fight-or-flight" response in his brain. So don't. Keep yourself busy with other projects so he doesn't get the impression that you're like a puppy dog desperately hankering after the "L" Word. Instead, reward him for all the nice things that he is doing for you. Don't make him feel that you need to hear those three little words or else. Honestly, saying "I love you" before he does is just, well . . . needy. And needy is far from attractive.

> **Fight-or-Flight Mode:** A man goes into fight-or-flight mode when he feels pressure to match your emotion and what you are feeling in the relationship. Innately, he knows that if he feels the "wrong" thing, he'll get punished. To get out of feeling what he doesn't want to, he'll pick a fight with you to buy him time, or he'll physically leave the situation and never call again.

2. Make Him Feel Safe

No matter how frustrated you are with your man, keep your cool. If you nag or threaten him to feel the same way that you do, he will feel pressure and get into fight-or-flight mode, which is never conducive to relationships because it can inadvertently make you into (gasp!) the enemy. And that doesn't make him feel safe.

When a man says "I love you" in a relationship, it's his way of telling you that he's willing to take the next step, be exclusive, and be faithful. There is no way in the world he's going to let down his guard and risk being rejected by you if he doesn't feel entirely safe, secure, and loved back, first. So yes, feel his love. And show your love before you even think of getting him to say the words. Make him realize he's got your trust.

3. Reinforce the Positive Associations He Has with You

Try this simple trick to put forth your best self to your man: Every time you answer his phone calls, have a big smile on your face. If you do that, your man will feel a sense of warmth and pleasantness when he answers the phone and therefore associate positive and happy feelings with his interactions with you. You can also answer the phone excitedly to let him know that you are happy to hear from him. You'll give him warm fuzzies every time you speak or are around each other. Certainly there is an element of performance to inspiring a man to do anything. And in fact, "acting as if" helps change your mood around instantly. When you smile, you actually release the "happy" chemical in your body, which can turn your mood around. Even on the most foul days, find something to smile about and you'll start feeling good again. Why? Because the human brain can only think one thought at a time. So you might as well make it pleasant! It's a win/win for everyone.

4. Remove Yourself from the Situation

Sometimes the best thing to do is just get away. It works wonders because distance really does make a man's heart grow fonder. If you're always around and make things easy for your man, he won't have to chase you and won't feel the challenge to hunt you down to claim you as his. When you feel that you're miles away from your man ever saying "I love you," remove yourself from the situation, your city, or his apartment, pronto. Serving yourself to him on a silver platter is the worst way to get a guy to declare his love. Remember, he's more inclined to say it when he thinks he's going to get a reward in return for taking that next step. If he's already getting rewards every second night (or twice a night!), he has zero motivation to tell you he loves you. He feels he's done enough because he's already getting the best of you!

Man Whisperers know how to "take away" from a man whom they feel isn't showing them enough love, lust, generosity —whatever. If you can't really get out of town, take a break in closer range. Don't call, text, or e-mail him for three to five days. Unless he calls you, and actually manages to get you on the phone, you are unavailable. Go out. Have a blast. Quite simply, don't spend hours at home thinking of him. In that sense, men are like dogs. They instinctively know when there's a change in the air . . . and if he loves you and wants to keep you, he'll do something about it! If you live with your man, find an activity that keeps you out of the house (one that doesn't mean coming home completely drunk!). Go see a museum opening, develop a new interest, or take a class. Break up the routine. And if you can, leave town. You'll both gain perspective. Keep it light. Going out shows him that you need more than the old routine to keep your interest. Ease him into it and explain that your cell phone will be off for most of the trip and you'll see him in a few days. And, of course, add that you are look- ing forward to seeing him. That way he won't get worried or instantly defensive.

> "When I need a total break from mar- riage and life, I take a vacation where the cell phone service is really bad. That way my husband doesn't take it personally when we don't speak for several days."
>
> —ELLY, 38, DENTAL HYGIENIST

5. Zip It and Practice Patience

Remember that Zipping It is an effective Man Whispering strategy. You're not being quiet or mousey. We know you are articulate and have plenty to say. But save your thousands of words for those afternoons when you're getting manicures with your girlfriends. Why? Because your man's problem-solving ability multiplies the minute you stop talking. For most women, patience isn't our set default. Nor is it second nature. That's why you must practice patience. Sometimes you have to wait for the response that you want. And when you do, men give truly from their hearts not just to restore the peace... and quiet!

Whispering to Hear "I Love You" More Often

When you're seriously committed or married, you've probably already heard "I love you" before. But once things are past the honeymoon "kissy-kissy" period, you might find yourself fed up that he doesn't say "I love you" *enough*. At that point, you need to learn another Man Whispering secret: figuring out his "love signs."

What Are Love Signs?

Believe it or not, for many men, telling women they "love" them has come to mean danger, commitment, and the very real possibility of rejection. So instead of taking the risk, men have come up with their own little code to declare their love for the object of their affection.

Men show their love by how generously they give and what they do for you, which is expressed in a myriad of ways—which we call love signs. You need to learn how to see the signs, recognize them, reward him for them, and make him feel appreciated.

Here are some common love signs:

- He calls and makes plans to see you
- He pays for dates
- He introduces you to family, friends, and work colleagues
- He gives generously during sex
- He takes care of your car
- He fixes things for you and tries to solve your problems
- He (mostly) willingly accompanies you to see the occasional chick flick
- He pays you compliments
- He is generous with spending time with you
- He honors the commitments he makes to you

Every time a man does something like that, he's showing you that he loves you. The words may not have come out of his mouth, but his actions speak for him. Once you realize all the ways that he *shows* you he loves you, you will no longer beg him to *say* "I love you" to you. You'll see it and be able to feel it without hearing it. You will be able to see his commitment to your relationship from an entirely different point of view. And as all Man Whisperers know best, the less you demand something of him, and the more you Zip It, the better!

Man Whispering Exercise

Keep a journal and write down the ways you believe your man tells you he loves you. Did he change your flat tire? Put gas in your car? Take you to your favorite restaurant? Tell you that you looked hot in that sexy new H&M mini you just bought? Did he call you when he said he would, or squeeze time in between meetings to send you a thoughtful text? Did he pay you a surprise visit? Ask how your grandmother was doing? Keep a list and you'll be amazed at how many times he shows his true affection without actually saying the words!

His love signs:

_____

_____

_____

_____

_____

_____

_____

_____

CASE STUDY: HEIDI AND JAMES

Heidi thought she found herself in a relationship devoid of the "L" Word. As a married woman in her early thirties, she was fed up that her husband no longer told her that he loved her. Nor did he show her much affection. She'd look longingly at other couples at the restaurant snuggling up to one another and couldn't quite understand why things in her marriage were so cold and distant. She eventually decided to just come right out and ask her husband.

Angrily, she told him this: "I'm always gushing to you about how much I love you. But you never just come up behind me, put your arms around me, and tell me you love me. Why is that?"

Her husband was shocked. "What do you mean, I don't tell you that I love you?" he replied. "Didn't I take you out for dinner the other night? Didn't I buy you that painting you liked for the living room? Didn't I help you fix your computer yesterday? You're always on my mind. Almost everything I do is for you."

Heidi was flabbergasted. All this time she'd been beating herself up over the fact that James didn't use words to declare his love for her, and yet here he was showing it and supporting her in myriad other ways!

He went on to remind Heidi that he supported her in opening up a new recruitment business, and that he would pay the first six months of her rent if she found an office space. This was his way of showing his love. James didn't say it with words. In fact, instead of "gushing," he showed her through his actions, which included being very generous with his financial resources.

Man Whispering Mantras
Chapter 7

- Never say "I love you" to him first—this puts a demand on him to say it back. It also triggers his fight-or-flight response.
- Don't act needy for his affections—Man Whisperers have it going on, and certainly enjoy a man's attention and affection, but don't rely upon it for their happiness.
- Don't let your oxytocin trick you into thinking you love the man you've just bonked, either. It's not you—it's your hormones that are making you feel this way. Think about it—especially if you've only just met the guy. How could you possible L-O-V-E him?
- Act independent but let him know that he is needed, appreciated, and wanted at the same time.
- Remove yourself from the situation: Tell him you're taking a surprise getaway, going out with girlfriends, or are going to a wedding alone. When he asks why, tell him you just need some time out and are looking forward to turning your phone off and having some girly time.
- Resist asking him flat-out to say that he loves you. Instead look at all the ways he's showing you his affection.
- If it's been way more than enough time for you, and still nothing, plus you've analyzed all the potential love signs and just aren't feeling it, then re-evaluate your situation. He may not be in love with you, and you deserve more than that! Don't force him to say it; just accept what it is and walk away if it's not what you want from your romantic relationship.

CHAPTER 8

Will He Ever Say "I Do"?

Get him to put a ring on your finger (without feeling like he's under lockdown)

"Marriage requires a special talent, like acting. Monogamy requires genius."
—WARREN BEATTY

"A woman's genius is learning to speak to his Monogamy Gene."
—DONNA AND SAM

First, Ask Yourself: Why Do I Want to Be Married?

It's not fair to your man that you insist he propose because you are bored, financially strapped, tired of being single, or have had enough of your mother's insistence that you settle down. If you're frantic to get engaged, figure out the real reasons behind your rush. Seriously, once you're past all the hullabaloo of announcing you're engaged, showing off your sparkling ring, buying the dress, walking down the aisle, and enjoying your honeymoon, the rush is over.

If you're in a hurry for the wrong reasons, don't push it. Women who simply want the fantasy of a fairy-tale wedding rather than the actual commitment to another person usually ask themselves, "That's it?" once they settle in post-wedding. If that happens to you, you'll soon be looking for the next relationship rush, which, like sugar, will spike and then crash.

Men Have Every Excuse in the Book

If you do want to get married for the right reasons, and would prefer your man not run with around with his secretary, his intern, your nanny, or your best friend, then you want to learn the whispering techniques to access and activate his Monogamy Gene. Yep, just like the female G spot, this elusive notion does indeed exist—you just need to know exactly what to do with it once you access it. And when you do, you'll learn what a man needs to keep his interest on you, and only you.

Of course, if you've dated for more than a nanosecond, you know by now that it's rare to hear a man lament that he is searching for "a relationship." Or that he wants to delay sex to see if he's really in love with a woman. Or that he so desperately wants kids that he's ready to "settle down" with the next half-decent woman who crosses his path. Not to mention the fact that men are notorious for giving anti-commitment excuses ranging from the fantastical to the incredibly nonsensical, all to ensure he gets into your pants quickly, cheaply, and without having to talk about rings, babies, wedding bells, or joint checking accounts.

Think your man's excuse for not committing is ridiculous? Wait till you hear these . . . Johnny Depp once claimed he didn't want to ruin his girlfriend's last name; Brad Pitt famously said he'll only get married "when everyone else in the country who wants to be married is legally able"; George Clooney said he's just "no good at it"; and our friend Ken says he'll "ruin the relationship" with a wedding.

Your man and his rampant anti-marriage excuses are not so unusual after all. Still, a woman can get mightily confused when she hears a friend tell her that she's demanding her man propose. Or she hears about a woman who cornered her man into admitting that he's the marrying type. Is that the best way to go about it? No, no, no!

The Top Reasons Men Are Afraid of Marriage

Clearly most men are resistant to the "M" Word. The best way to deal with your man's greatest fears is to try to assure him they won't come to pass. So, it's time to do some sleuthing. Figure out what your man's deepest fears of commitment are—is he afraid you'll prevent him from playing poker, redecorate his apartment in chartreuse, or that you'll stop having sex with him, or quit being your kind, loving, fun self?—and then allay them. Don't laugh at him, either. Often, a person's deepest fears are irrational and don't make logical sense. In the realm of emotions, rationality rarely shows its face. So be patient and supportive if his fears seem silly to you. They aren't silly to him, and they may be the only thing that's keeping him from popping the question. So don't shoot yourself in the ring finger! Here are some reasons men might be afraid of commitment:

They're Afraid They Won't Have a Lot of Sex Anymore

Men think single life equals loads of sex, while getting hitched means pulling the plug on good or frequent sex forever. With magazines highlighting sexless marriages and entire television shows committed to helping sexless couples get their mojos back, it's no wonder men live in grave fear that walking down the aisle means the end of the hanky-panky as they know it.

There's a famous scene from the movie *Wedding Crashers* where serial womanizer John Beckwith finds the groom puking in the bathroom before the wedding. John then details exactly what was running through the groom's head: the end to his sex life and the end of him.

Men have a gazillion reasons for refusing to commit, even when they deeply love you. Which is why you need to whisper to him that you won't stifle his lifestyle, his freedom, or stop having sex with him once the two of you get hitched. Once you get that message across to him, you'll be well on your way to matrimony.

They're Afraid of Losing Their Identities

Another top fear men have about getting married is the fear of losing themselves. Your man is worried that the minute he proposes, his life and his identity as he knows and loves it is over.

Other Reasons He Might Be Afraid

1. He's afraid that you'll spend all his money, still not be satisfied, and want more, more, and more.
2. He's afraid he'll give you everything he has and you'll leave him for another man.
3. He's afraid you'll turn off sexually and he'll be a desperate and lonely man deprived of sex.
4. He's afraid that you'll change and become unattractive to him.
5. He's afraid that once you have kids, you'll focus all your love on the children and ignore him.
6. He's afraid of getting stuck to the point where leaving the relationship is too difficult or expensive, so he will stay and suffer a lifetime of misery.

So what's a Man Whisperer to do? Allay his fears. If he's worried about money, show him how budget-conscious you are. If he's worried about physical appearances, show him how dedicated you are to staying healthy and in good shape. If he's worried about becoming bored, demonstrate variety so that he knows you'll always stay interesting to him. And so on.

Here are some specific things you can casually say to help address his fears:

- While making him groan with pleasure, say, "Oh, this? This is nothing, I have more tricks up my G-string."
- When he's initiating sex, say, "I was dreaming about you touching me here all day."
- When he's doing something mundane like watching TV, suddenly fan yourself like you're getting hot and say, "I get so turned on just looking at you."
- While getting dressed, say, "Is this skirt short enough for you? Or should I wear the micro-mini tonight?"
- When hearing about women going for a man's jugular in a divorce say, "I don't understand why women have to be so cruel and take a man for every penny his has. It's just not right."
- While making plans for the week, say to him, "Honey, do you think we spend enough time apart doing our own thing?"
- When giving him a blowjob, say, "I love this. I could do this forever!"
- While balancing the checkbook say, "How about we shake up our routine? Want to save up for a surf trip or that motorcycle ride you've been talking about?"
- When showing him your new clothes, say, "I waited until it was on sale for half-price." Or, "I don't feel comfortable spending too much on clothes. Just enough to feel pretty and look good for you."
- While on the phone, end the conversation by saying, "Babe, I'm off to the gym to keep my tush looking hot for you."

In time, your man will register these comments, and they will go a long way toward easing his specific fears.

Commitment Has to Be His Choice

Once you've addressed his fears about marriage, your man is likely to come to a decision to propose all on his own. And that's exactly the situation you want. To demand anything from a man is to breach Man Whisperer Mantras, especially when it relates to monogamy, marriage, or anything to do with scoring a Harry Winston diamond. Whispering offers a solution. It allows your man to take action based on inspiration—because you set it up in a way so that whatever he suggests is his brilliant idea. That way, when he offers you a commitment, it was because he wanted to, not because you pressured him into it.

ALERT! *Why Men Stay Single*

According to the U.S. Census Bureau, the number of men who are single has significantly increased since 1990. The number one reason why men these days stay single? Because—surprise, surprise—they can get sex without marriage more easily than ever before. A study done at Rutgers University in 2002 found that men believe they can get hot action in the bedroom without even paying for dinner, and that bonk buddies are fast becoming a single man's best friend. Most men say that they consider the women they meet in bars and at dance clubs as casual sex partners rather than marriage material.

> "My girlfriend complains that I 'never' call her. She continually calls me and asks 'where is this going?' She wants to know everything up-front and says I'm a commitmentphobe because I haven't asked her to marry me. But guess what? I don't have commitmentphobia! And actually, I was going to propose. But I feel so badgered that I'm turned off. And I'm afraid of what else she is going to badger me about. It's kaput because with a woman like that, demands only get worse."
>
> —DON, 32, REAL ESTATE AGENT

Don is like most guys we speak to: He's fed up with the way women demand commitment, sex, and money and insist that men answer their questions immediately. And who can blame him? What you might not know is that Don, like many men, really is interested in finding a woman who will make him want to settle down. He lives in hope that he'll meet someone he'll want to take home and introduce to his mother. But instead, all his girlfriends speak straight to his Anti-Monogamy Gene and scare him off. They mistakenly believe that pressuring him is the key to weaving their way into Don's heart. No such luck. Nevertheless, these women continue to call and chase Don until eventually he tells them that he's "just not ready for a relationship." Then they scoff, pout, and bitch to all their friends that Don is clearly a commitmentphobe with major issues.

Yet the truth is, he's desperate to find a good woman he can commit to—he just doesn't want the pressure. He wants it to be his choice; a choice he will make when he's ready to do so. Don says that it's becoming more and more difficult to find a woman he can adore, cherish, and see as the father of his children . . . and also is a woman who lets him chase her.

The Importance of the Chase

To learn how to Man Whisper to his Monogamy Gene, first you need to understand the cycle of love. Let's go back to Don. When Don sees a gorgeous girl by the bar with spilling cleavage and smoldering blue eyes, his dopamine levels instantly rise. This tells his brain that the hunt is on. Don's brain will now place all his focus and attention on the woman he desires until the hunt is won . . . and over. His biological instincts tell him that he needs to do everything in his power to bed her that very night. So the chase begins. He finds out her name is Kendra. He buys her a drink, tells her his funniest joke, gently touches her hair, says something delectable into her ear, actually listens when she talks, and tries to ask her all the right questions.

> **Monogamy Gene:** Men want sex as cheaply as they can get it. But they also want a home and a family, and have the desire to build a family and a legacy with the right woman. This is their Monogamy Gene. Address this side of him and he'll desire settling down with you more than fooling around with other women.

Don knows that it's usually at this point in the night that women agree to come back to his place—or may even suggest it themselves. But wait; Kendra is different. She giggles when he invites her back to his place and tells him it's too soon and she's got an early-morning Pilates class. But she would love to see him another time. For lunch. Kendra knows that if they did have sex that night, Don's dopamine levels would drop to almost zero (until he gets horny again!) and the chase would be over. This is because when he gets his prey and she gives him an orgasm, he releases the hormones oxytocin and vasopressin, which will actually block the dopamine (what causes him to chase her) in his brain.

ALERT! *Extend the Chase*

According to Ted Huston at the University of Texas at Austin, the speed at which courtship progresses often determines the ultimate success of the relationship. The longer the courtship, the stronger the long-term relationship. The study, which looked at the success rate of 168 marriages since 1979, found that happily married couples dated for twenty-five months, while couples who rushed intimacy due to events such as moving in together or becoming pregnant didn't last as long. That's why you never want to rush sex or make demands for premature commitment.

This first-meet example is an important lesson for women who have been with a man for a while and want him to continue to pursue her and slip a ring on her finger. Even when you find a man you like, and are in a relationship with him, slow it down, ladies. There's no rush! Relish the chase for him to make you his forever. Remember those pre-sex days when you and your beau would cuddle and kiss and touch for hours? Then once you had sex, you were left wondering what happened to all the kissing. It is important to enjoy every phase of your relationship because when you're creating positive memories together, you are strengthening your bond. Don't make the mistake of wanting to fast forward to "I do." It is this slowing down of the chase that encourages him to make you his forever.

Instead, Kendra stays at the bar with her girlfriends and lets Don go home alone. She knows that if he is serious, he will go to bed thinking of her. The positive hormones will still be coursing throughout his body for days and he'll be more inclined to call her the next day, and the next. She isn't playing games; she's simply whispering to his biological chemical makeup. She is doing what women are supposed to do: wait until SHE decides whether or not she likes a guy. While she's busy making her decision, she's allowing his chemical reactions to do what they're designed to do: build up to such an intense pace that suddenly Don will see her as someone he must have, even if that means he must be monogamous (and suppress his animal anti-monogamy instincts) to keep her.

This is a process you want to repeat for as long as your relationship lasts. You want to keep this up for as long as you are together. It's this inner steadiness that will keep men "chasing you" even when you've been together for decades.

How to Get Him to Propose Before You Move in with Him

Let's say Kendra's plan works like a charm. When she decides that Don has proved himself to be a worthy partner, she agrees to spend the night at his house. What follows is a magical, electrifying night to remember. After a few months of dating, Don begs Kendra to move in with him. They live forty-five minutes away from one another and the commute is killing them both. Kendra has her own life and a busy career, so she hasn't been able to make as much time for Don as she would like. Don figures that he really likes this woman and wants to see if they might potentially work long-term. He continues to beg Kendra to move in and Kendra surmises that a bigger apartment, less rent, and someone to help with the dishes might not be such a bad idea after all. She's really fallen for Don and thinks that if they're going to take the next step, it might as well be now. But she knows that it's dangerous to move in with a man before a sign of actual commitment to marriage—namely a ring.

> ## ALERT! *The Case for Living Separately until Marriage*
> A Columbia University study found there's actually less chance of marrying a person when you live with them, with only 26 percent of women and a scant 19 percent of the men surveyed marrying the person they cohabited with. The survey showed that partners who live together before marriage are nine times more likely to split up than those who get married first.

Yet Kendra isn't sure she's ready to get engaged and she doesn't want to rush things either. Nor does she want to be in a position whereby all her stuff is moved into Don's place, they have a fight, and she's left homeless. (She knows other women who have found themselves in that exact predicament.) She still wants to speak to his Monogamy Gene and doesn't want to blow things, because she is interested in him as a future husband. But she knows that if she moves in without receiving a concrete commitment from him first, she runs the risk of being left with nothing. So she follows this Man Whispering recipe.

1. She removes herself from the situation (by not coming over to his place too often and by sweetly deflecting his offers to move in).
2. She states how she is feeling or gives an observation. For example, she says things like, "Honey, this commute is so far, but it's worth it to see you." Or, "I totally see us living together one day. But it's important to me to know that the arrangement isn't just a matter of convenience but of commitment. And we may not be ready for that."
3. She Zips It. She does not blame him or herself for this situation.
4. She lets him fix it by proposing when the time is right for him.

Realize That He Has Plans and Feelings, Too!

Sometimes women are so concerned with their own life plans that they forget to include their men in them. It shouldn't be surprising that this sets up another barrier to commitment. For example, twenty-eight-year-old Michelle's relationships never seemed to last . . . and she was mightily flummoxed as to why. She'd been dating Gary for two years and constantly tells him of her plans to get married, have babies, and move to the suburbs. In fact, the minute she met Gary, she laid all her cards out on the table. She thought she was just being up-front with him about what she wanted, but now she cannot understand why he seems to be pulling further and further away. When Michelle approached us for a solution to her unmarried woes, we asked her to paint us a picture as to what had transpired prior to Gary's deflection of her marriage plans.

Man Whisperers: So, when did you first tell Gary about all these plans?

Michelle: Oh, within the first two weeks! I'm not wasting my time with a man who doesn't have the same goals as me. Why should I? My clock is ticking. Why should I have to wait?

MW: Wait?! You're giving the poor guy a heart attack! You're pushing him into a corner. He feels like you're locking him up permanently. As much as he may love you, no man wants that! But men do want a loving wife who they can spend fun-filled days with. If you see yourself as that type of woman, then whisper to him that this is the type of woman you are!

Gary came to us separately from Michelle. He asked us why some women seem to have their lives all mapped out, and just expect a man to jump right in. He felt like more of a sperm donor and an ATM machine than a lover, best friend, potential husband, and father.

"It's like they don't care who the man is," he said. "Some women today just have their plan and they just need some guy—any guy—to slot right in."

The good news for Michelle was that she really did love Gary and so she was willing to do something differently. She softened and started to see Gary as a person who had his own hopes, dreams, and fears instead of simply as a means to her end. She focused on their complementary aspects, whispered to plant the seeds of marriage, and watched them grow. And most important, she Zipped It. She did not make any further mention of marriage and her ticking clock. Instead, she used her words to paint a serene picture of what life with her would be like in the future. And it worked! The more Michelle changed her behavior, the more Gary turned around.

Cardinal Faux Pas for Whispering to His Monogamy Gene

As you go through the process of making him feel comfortable with commitment, many women are tempted to fall into certain common traps. Here are four such no-no's to avoid at all costs.

Faux Pas #1: Being Too Needy

If you try desperately to get your man to commit, you turn (in his eyes) into a bunny-boiling psychopath who is trying to cramp his style and close him in. A continuous stream of phone calls, text messages, invitations, and outings with your folks (and temper tantrums if he wants to see his mates) is enough to make him all but run away to the desert to remain celibate for all eternity. Being needy is being demanding. Don't be that woman!

ALERT! *Don't Give Away the Milk . . .*

Sex never guarantees commitment, and especially never guarantees a ring. A woman needs to learn to first receive what she wants from a man; only then can she decide if she wants to give him what he wants (which is usually sexual pleasure). While this may sound a little old-fashioned, if you've tried it the other way around and it hasn't worked for you, what do you have to lose by keeping your sexual cards and marital goals closer to your heart? Try changing your tactics next time. From now on, receive what you want from a man *before* you give him what he wants.

Faux Pas #2: Pretending You Never Want to Settle Down

Modern women have been warned not to come on too strong and to revel in their singlehood. Yet some have taken this go-girl feminist mantra to another level. Instead of the equally "ready for marriage yesterday" gal who continually hints at marriage and forces her boyfriend to go shopping for a wedding ring, this new type of woman *pretends* she doesn't want to commit (ever!) and vehemently denies the fact that she ever wants to walk down the aisle or have babies anytime soon. But alas, she may be in a relationship with a guy who is wondering if there is a future with her. Before you can shout "hear me roar," he's off trying to find himself someone who can envision herself taking the next steps in a relationship. Trying to out-commitmentphobe a commitmentphobe doesn't work. This type of reverse logic won't get a man to commit.

Faux Pas #3: Trying to Change Your Man

There is nothing that scares a man away faster (aside from Broadway tickets to *Legally Blonde*) than a woman who wants to change him. When his sense of style, the way he refuses to put gel in his hair, or the amount of time he spends with his friends is judged, criticized, nitpicked, and disparaged, you can be guaranteed he'll instantly transform into a commitmentphobe—to get away from you. Again, this does not mean that your man will never change—you can use whispering techniques to show him what would please you. But you absolutely cannot force it to happen by sheer will or by nagging. It won't work and will only push him away.

Faux Pas #4: Suffering from the "Be Like Me" Syndrome

Some women believe that once they're in a relationship, their man must become just like them. So she attempts to turn him into a Pilates-going, tofu-eating, chick-flick-loving guy who isn't allowed to drink beer, play football with his friends, or—gasp—ogle other women. To be complementary in a relationship means that you must be different. So *vive la différence!* Let him be himself so you can find out who he is. Only then can you know if he's the right guy for you.

Man Whispering to Get Him to Propose

Once you have laid the groundwork of making sure you want to get married for the right reasons and then easing your man's fears of marriage, you can begin whispering specifically to get him to propose. When you are certain the time is right, do the following:

1. Make a suggestion or observation about how you feel: "I'm really excited for my future and I feel it's time for me to move to the next phase of my life. I'm going to give this X more months/weeks/days (insert timeline and level of commitment) before I will have to move on."
2. Zip It.
3. Remove yourself from the situation.
4. Wait for him to fix it.

If his solution to your statement pleases you, go with it. If it doesn't, be prepared to move on. It's that simple. (We're not saying it's *easy* to move on; just that the process is simple once you've decided what you want from the relationship.)

CASE STUDY: ROSELLA AND TOM

Rosella and Tom had been in a committed relationship for more than six years. They met in college and had been steady and faithful ever since. They were now living together in a beautiful apartment right on the beach. The problem was that for the last year, they had been growing apart and their relationship was simply limping along. Rather than berate Tom for all the things he was doing wrong and point out all the ways he was failing to please her, Rosella simply stated what she needed. "Tom," she said, "I feel that we've come to a point in our relationship where we either need to deepen our commitment to each other and become engaged or I need to move out."

While on the surface it may seem like she had given him an ultimatum, she wasn't saying it was over. She was simply letting him know her needs to remain in the relationship. Then she Zipped It and allowed Tom the time and the peace to mull it over and understand more deeply his level of commitment to her and their relationship. Rosella also removed herself from the situation and packed a bag and stayed at a friend's house. In the next two weeks, Rosella found an apartment and put down a deposit. She gently communicated her move-in date to Tom.

Of course, this process was painful at best. But Rosella was communicating to Tom, in gentle, loving language and clear terms, what she required from him to stay living together. Two days before her move-out date, Tom invited Rosella on a hike. With the view of the Pacific Ocean in front of them, he pulled out a ring from his backpack, bent down on one knee, and asked Rosella to marry him. She said, "Yes!" They now have been married for twelve years and have two adorable kids.

Rosella didn't think that Tom should know magically how she felt. She also didn't expect him to jump into his decision quickly and didn't hold it against him when it took him three (albeit extremely painful and tear-filled) weeks to realize he didn't want to lose her and become ready to do what she requested of him to keep her. As Tom's friends said, "In three weeks, he became a man."

The Hidden Price of Threatening Ultimatums

Both women and men are called to action either by pain or inspiration. Usually women give ultimatums when they are in so much pain in a relationship that they finally "stick up for themselves" and communicate their needs to their man. But now, instead of it being wrapped in a Man Whispering bow, it's a do-or-die ultimatum. That ultimatum calls him into action by pain and infers a demand that he respond to you in the gun-to-his-head sort of way.

When a man gives in to an ultimatum, there is a hidden price: deep resentment. If you push him into the corner with an ultimatum, he is faced with two painful decisions . . . do what you ask to continue the relationship (although he may or may not be ready), or go through the pain of losing you.

Sure, you may get a man to commit to you this way, but why would you when there is a better and easier way that leverages his innate desire to please you?

Man Whispering Mantras
Chapter 8

- Know the reason why your man is delaying commitment, and then address the reason with your actions and proving him wrong. Whisper to him that you won't stifle his lifestyle or his freedom or stop having sex with him once the two of you get hitched.
- Always let a man chase you, rather than the other way around. That way you'll capture his heart for life, rather than just for a few minutes in the sack.
- Don't move in with a man before he proposes or there is at least a promise of a ring. While this might sound old-fashioned, statistics prove that your relationship has less of a chance of succeeding in the long run if you live with him before you're married. If you have nowhere to go, move in with a friend or a family member. A romantic relationship is not meant to solve your economic crisis.
- Never give a man a marriage ultimatum. Instead, be the type of woman he desperately wants to marry!

The Emotionally Available Male

Goodbye, Mr. Macho;
Hello, Mr. Generous!

"Men expect too much, do too little."
—ALLEN TATE

*"Man Whispering helps men open up . . .
their hearts and their wallets."*
—DONNA AND SAM

Dealing with a Man Who's Emotionally Unavailable

Ever dated a man who's emotionally unavailable? You know, the type who freaks out if you try to talk about anything that resembles his heart—and instead runs to the nearest driving range with headphones and an endless number of golf balls? This frustrating scenario can be undone, however—let Man Whispering show you the way!

Kibosh His Fear of Inadequacy

Insecurity is one of the biggest causes of emotionally unavailability. Men are more insecure than you think. In fact, one of his biggest fears is that he'll become a failure. A failure with money; in the boardroom; in the bedroom; with his kids; and in the eyes of his wife, his father, and colleagues—the list goes on and on! So how do you ease his fears of failure? How do you inspire him to open up, let you in, and share his problems with you?

You massage his ego, that's how. Yep, the key to a man's heart isn't in his stomach. It lies in his self-esteem. Boost it the right way, and he'll love you more than you love a half-off shoe sale. In fact, how well you whisper to his ego can make all the difference between a decent relationship and an amazing one.

ALERT! *Egos Matter*

It happens all the time: Men with beautiful, talented wives or girlfriends cheat on them with women whom most men wouldn't touch with a ten-foot pole. The reason? She boosts his ego. These women know how to make a man feel special and necessary. They fluff his man feathers and make him feel like he's the most important person on the planet. Don't let your man go searching for that chick! Whisper to him every day just how special and important he is to you and your family. It's good for you too, as it makes you appreciate his positives, and whatever you appreciate grows.

Quick Ways to Whisper to His Ego

Now that you know that some of his emotional unavailability is caused by his fears of inadequacy, you can address those fears by giving him sincere compliments frequently. If you truly can't find anything to compliment him on, then, why are with him in the first place? Second, don't fake it. Insincerity will not work to your advantage. Man Whispering is not about manipulation or falsely leading a man on. It's about being genuine and bringing out the best qualities in your man—the ones that already exist and just need a little bit of a polish. Here's how to whisper some compliments that get to the root of men's common hang-ups:

- **His body:** Tell him that he has great arms, nice pecs, or that you love his hairy chest. Focus on something that he's proud of, or that you personally find irresistibly sexy.
- **His skills:** Whether it be the way he barbecued the lamb roast, his ability to fix the computer, or his tenacity for golf—tell him how proud you are that he is so good at that skill. (Especially if it's one that benefits you— because he'll want to do it more often!)
- **His personality:** Does he always call his mother? Is he kind to strangers? Is he doting around babies? Is he a loyal friend? All these character traits are important to notice in your man. Start looking for the good in his personality and shine a light on it.
- **His strength:** Whatever his strength in life is—whether it's always being on time, or his passion for working out and eating healthy—let him know that you appreciate it and that it turns you on.
- **His sexual prowess:** Never tell him that someone else was better in bed or that you faked an orgasm. If you find that he's not fulfilling you in the bedroom, skip to Chapter 12. But if you find that he's like a seasoned pro beneath the sheets, tell him. Then tell him again in a cheeky e-mail or text message the following day. Or, even better, tell him over lunch or dinner, or whisper it into his ear at a restaurant.
- **His hobbies:** Whether it be his passion for sports cars, guitars, or collecting stamps, whatever it is, support it. Let him know that you're not going to take the "boy-hood" lollipop out of his mouth.
- **His, ahem, assets:** Compliment him in front of your girlfriends or his friends, as subtly as possible. You don't want to embarrass him, but at the same time he'll be as proud as can be.

"My girlfriend once said that I was 'stacked' in front of her friends. Although that comment made me blush, secretly I loved her for it."

—SIMON, 29, WEB DESIGNER

Boosting his ego in these ways will help you put him at ease enough to feel like he can open up emotionally with you.

CASE STUDY: MARIE AND TIM

Marie, a successful litigator, describes the day she was at the beach with her boyfriend, Tim, who had set up an elaborate beach camp for her and all her friends to enjoy. At the end of the day when they were packing up, her boyfriend looked like a mule piled high with all sorts of beach chairs, towels, and a cooler on the half-mile hike back up to the car. As they walked up, one of Marie's friends was aghast. "Aren't you going to help him?"

Marie replied, "Of course! Tim asked me to carry this," and she lifted a dinky shopping bag full of left-over potato chips. Marie's friend's face was full of shock and she rushed up to help Marie's boyfriend. Marie stopped her.

"Listen," she said, "It makes him feel good that he's doing all the heavy lifting. He wants it this way. He likes it. It gives him a sense of masculinity and boosts his ego."

Marie's friend shook her head in disbelief. She couldn't get over Marie not wanting to be equal and carry "her half." But Marie understood that lugging all the heavy beach stuff made her man feel like her hero. And Marie was looking forward to giving his big man muscles a massage for all the heavy lifting he did all day. Instead of carrying "her half," Marie knew the magic of being complementary with her man. That way he can be her hero for the day and she could reward him with her praise and attention.

Encourage Him to Drop His Guard

While it's rather simple to boost a man's ego (just tell him how good he was in bed the night before and he'll be glowing for days!), it's a whole different ballgame when it comes to getting him to express his feelings. The cows will come home before a man will willingly drop his guard and open up about his inner thoughts. The "F" word—feelings—does not exist in his vocabulary. Or at least he pretends it doesn't.

If you ask your man how he's feeling at the end of a hard week, despite the fact you know he's down in the dumps, has just lost his job, or had a fight with his best buddy, he'll reply with a terse, "I'm fine." Remember, as women, we want to talk about it. And talk about it some more. But men are hardwired differently. They don't want to talk about it. They want to blow off steam alone. And if they are angry, they want to drain the raging testosterone pumping through their veins some other way.

Once you sense something is wrong with your man, let him blow off steam first. Don't expect him to talk about it *now*. Let him know that you're concerned and available to talk when and if he wants to, then leave it at that. Take a look at these two examples of communication.

Non-Whisperers:
NMW: "How was your work meeting?"
Him: "Pretty crappy."
NMW: "Why? What happened? Did you lose the account?"
Him: "It just was! Okay?! Can't I get some peace around here?"

Whisperers:
MW: "How was your work meeting?"
Him: "Pretty crappy."
MW: "Sorry to hear that, baby."

Then give him a squeeze and tell him something short and sweet like, "I love you" and . . . Zip It. Perhaps even leave the room or your apartment/house. Most men need to blow off steam before they can ever open up about something. And they don't want us around when they punch a wall or kick a tire. Wait for it. You'll get the full story later.

Here's another example:

Non-Whisperers:
Him: "I can't help you with that today."
NMW: "Why not? You said you would. What's wrong? Tell me."
Him: "Because I just can't!"

Whisperers:
Him: "I can't help you with that today."
MW: "Hmmm. Okay. What would be a better day for me to ask you?"
OR
MW: "When would suit you better?"

OR

MW: "Will you let me know when you think is a good day?"

Usually, when a woman asks a man to discuss his feelings or share a problem, he will instantly put up his defenses. Instead of asking him "why" he feels a certain way (never a good idea!), or berating him for not opening up or being willing to talk about his feelings, approach it another way. For example:

Whisperers:

Him: "I don't want to talk about it."

MW: "That's okay. If you ever do, I'm here. Love you, babe."

OR

MW: "Is there something I can do—book you a massage, make you a grilled cheese sandwich, or go for a walk with you to clear your head?"

These Man Whisperer communication techniques show compassion but also give a man plenty of space to deal with his emotions in a way that's comfortable for him. His decision may not be most comfortable for you—after all, the woman in you wants to hear every little detail and dissect it—but this problem is not about you. Your man should solve it the way he wants.

Whispering to Get Your Man to Open Up

One you've made it clear that you're concerned about his problem, and you've given him time and space to deal with it, it's safe to take things to the next level to encourage him to share more with you. Remember, never ask him about his feelings—instead ask him to relay events when he's ready. You'll be able to deduce his feelings by tone of voice and the words he uses to describe what happened. And if you need further verification, go ahead and straight out ask, "Did that make you feel (insert feeling)?" That lets him either agree or disagree with a yes or no answer that you can home in on more clearly. Here are the guidelines to encourage him to share some emotions with you.

Rule 1: Timing Is Everything

Wait for the right time to bring it up. A man is not going to open up to you exactly when you want him to. You can bet your designer stilettos that he's not going to commiserate or open up when his focus is elsewhere—like when the game is on, or when he's playing online poker. Instead, broach the topic with him away from any big distractions. Before you dive in, first bargain for his time and wait until his focus is on you.

CASE STUDY: NANCY AND JOEL

Joel's father had just passed away and although Joel's eyes would tear over occasionally, his lips were as tight as a clam. He hadn't said a word about it to his wife, Nancy, but he was clearly hurting. For a few days, Nancy let him do his thing, knowing he needed time to deal with his emotions.

But on the third day, she made him his favorite dinner. As she poured him a glass of wine, she said, "Joel, do you mind if I ask you how you're doing? You look so sad. I'm here for you, baby." For Joel, it was like she just pulled the stopper out of the emotional dam. He still didn't say much, but he did tell her that he was having a rough time dealing with the loss. Nancy then sat in his lap and nuzzled him while Joel's tears silently flowed. Sometimes whispering to your man has more to do with showing him comfort than talking.

Rule 2: Listen!

When you're talking, you're not listening. This is a hard one to remember, but if you keep interrupting him, most likely he will retreat into his infamous man cave far, far away. Instead, Zip It and give him the space to gather his thoughts and speak his mind. This freedom lets him know that when he opens his mouth, he won't be judged or interrupted. Also, when he finally has decided to open up, be attentive. This is not the time to multitask. Get off your phone, put down the paper, stop surfing the Internet. If there's silence within the conversation, don't jump in to fill it with words and more words. In the silence, he's processing his thoughts—so let him.

Rule 3: Don't Attack Him

If you've kindly asked him if the two of you can chat, and you've bargained for his time and he's finally opening up to you, you've just created a wonderfully safe No-Attack Zone for him! You've done all this work to set up this zone; now isn't the time to start spouting off about how he *really* screwed up this time. Start by pointing out all the things he's done right. And then try using open-ended statements like, "What do you think about. . . ." Avoid starting sentences with, "How come you never . . ." and don't compare him to your best friend's husband or your next-door neighbor, either. He'll shut off emotionally and won't open up again, because he thinks that if he does, you'll punish him.

Rule 4: Don't Judge Him

This isn't an episode of *The People's Court* or *Judge Judy*. Even if you know that he was entirely wrong when it comes to his actions, Zip It at first and wait for an invitation from him for your advice. If he's telling you about a fight he had at work or an altercation with one of his family members, he's finally letting down his guard with you, so don't be so quick to judge the poor fellow! Otherwise, he'll probably never want to talk to you openly again.

Wait for him to finish and then ask him why he thought it was a good idea to behave that way, or what he thinks he got out of it. When people have made a mistake, they will usually come to their own conclusion that they did something wrong. You don't have to be the one to ram it down his throat. That's not the whispering way.

Rule 5: Open Up to Get Him to Open Up

Tell him something personal about yourself. If you know he had a rough childhood and it's tough for him to talk about it, tell him something about your own childhood. Make him realize that he's not the only one with a dysfunctional family, asshole coworker, or embarrassing teenage years. And make him feel that he can trust you because you are in the same boat he's in, and won't judge him on what he's about to tell you.

Rule 6: Remind Him That Neither One of You Has to Always Be Perfect

Make a rule in your relationship that it's okay to fail. If you fail at something, you can admit that, or that you were disappointed in the way you conducted yourself. Make it okay to be less than perfect. That way, he won't feel the pressure to always put on a brave front in front of you and will instead be encouraged to admit that he's wrong, rather than always trying to prove that he was right.

Rule 7: Pull Back

The power of Zipping It will serve you well while getting your man to open up. Too many women continue to ask, "What's bothering you?" "What can't you talk about it?" and "What's wrong with you?" The men complain that if their women would only stop asking them questions, they might actually get the chance to process and then share their thoughts.

Rule 8: Don't Offer a Solution Without His Asking for Your Advice

Remember a man thinks that he's the "fixer." He needs to be the one processing the information and then coming up with a solution. It needs to be *his* brilliant idea. He needs to figure out what he's going to do about it. The minute you trump this instinct, he thinks that you've lost faith in him. Which is why we whisper solutions to men: so they think they came up with them.

Rule 9: TLC Goes a Long Way

If he's had a bad day at work, or doesn't want to open up to you about something, accept his decision and just let him know that you are there for him. Show him you care by giving him what he loves: food, hugs, a compliment, and love and affection. Then leave him alone. Pop your head in every few hours just to let him know you are there and willing to listen, but keep busy with your own life. Wait for him to come to you.

> ALERT! *Don't Skimp on the Compliments*
> Many women we know often complain that their men don't notice their new hairstyles or new designer shoes. But did you know that according to a Yahoo.com article by David Zinczenko, editor-in-chief of *Men's Health*, nearly 70 percent of men say that they wish they received more compliments from their partners? So while you're busy complaining that your man doesn't compliment you enough, try saving that energy and throw a few compliments back on him.

How to Man Whisper to His Wallet and His Time

As we mentioned earlier, men feel that they are committing their money when they commit to an exclusive relationship with you. And clearly, you'll be the person he spends most of his time with. Both of these things can make him uneasy, defensive, and closed off. Here are some tactics to get him to open up.

Get Him to Open His Wallet

A friend of ours once said, "If my husband opened his wallet, a moth would fly out." If your man is similar, you might find yourself frustrated every time you have to deal with paying for something.

Of course, in today's world, women are almost equal to men in sheer numbers in the workforce. Men have become mightily tight with their money—and it's not becoming. So instead of treating us to meals (even when they invite us out!) or offering to give the cab driver a tip, many expect women to pay up. Many women are outraged. Men are more confused than ever before, and it's not entirely their fault. Although some women believe that since they buy their own diamonds, they can pay their own dinner bill, they still want a chivalrous man at heart. The trouble is that men think simply that because women make money (sometimes more than him, perhaps), women should be responsible for paying for their share of whatever they do.

> "My boyfriend's first gift to me was some pretty cheap perfume. But after I appreciated the heck out of it and clued him on what I really like, his gifts got much better."
> —JANICE, 28, FINANCIAL ANALYST

But Man Whispering is all about your happiness. And most women are happiest when a man is generous with her, as it's a clear sign that he is pleased to be in her company. And we're not talking about him spending a ridiculous amount of money on her either. Even if he doesn't have two cents to his name, it's about him saving up a few dollars to take her to his favorite sandwich shop and then to a beautiful seaside view to enjoy their meal together by the ocean. Romantic and thoughtful?

Yes. Expensive? Not at all. When we say a man needs to be generous, we're not talking about him flashing tons of cash. We're talking about being generous with his money at whatever level is appropriate.

As Hollywood actress Jessica Alba recently mused: "Guys should treat women with respect. I am still lady-like and feminine, but unfortunately a lot of men have lost their sense of chivalry. I like a man to open doors and offer to pay. But by no means do I need him to pay for things or tell me what I should or shouldn't do. I wouldn't like that. I'll have the children and be a wife, but I'm also going to work." So how do you keep that wallet of his open? You do the following:

- Show appreciation even in advance.
- Mention the times he was very generous, and be affectionate with him when you talk about it.
- Tell him how good it makes you feel when he takes care of the bill—that you feel like he's taking care of you. For example: "Thank you so much for taking me to a wonderful dinner . . . you make me feel so taken care of!"
- Notice the details when he does buy you something (and don't return it, even if it's not your color!)

It's smart to make a first impression that your life is exciting, fun, and something that your man will enjoy being a part of. And then keep that image going. You are in demand and going to fabulous restaurants, art openings, and wonderful parties. When he sees that you are a woman on the go, he'll chase you to keep up! So thrilled in fact, that he will open up his wallet (or save his weekly earnings) to be able to take you out. It's that simple. And the more you appreciate what he gives, the more he gives. But beware of overloading on designer brands to the point that you look like a billboard. Men we've interviewed have told us that the minute they see an entire wardrobe made up of clothing by Louis Vuitton, Chanel, Prada, Gucci, or Pucci, they fear you'll send him straight to the poorhouse. Your girlfriends may find it attractive, but he does not. Remember, everything in moderation. And men don't fall in love with you because you are dripping with diamonds. They fall in love with who you are and how you make them feel.

Dating and relationship expert Cherry Norris, who founded

> "When my husband made a few dollars an hour at a construction site when he was young, he spent it all on me!"
>
> —CINDY, 29, NUTRITIONIST

the successful dating seminar "How to Meet and Marry Your Man" in Los Angeles, reminds us that being wealthy doesn't mean a man will be generous. In fact, if you've dated around, you know all too well that some of the wealthiest men are also the stingiest. They'll ask you to split the bill and still want to have sex with you. They'll request that you pay for the valet parking and then split the cost of a cocktail. A truly generous man will pick up the tab (if he invited!). Your appreciation of his generosity is all he needs to give you even more.

CASE STUDY: LANA AND SIMON

When beautician Lana went on a date with banker Simon, they headed to one of New York's most expensive restaurants (his decision; his invitation). When the bill came, he just sat there with his arms folded. Luckily, Lana owned her own business and made loads of cash. So she decided to put the money on the table for her half. After all, it was early on in their relationship and she didn't want to seem like a gold digger. When he didn't make any attempt to reach for his wallet, she put the entire amount on the table and then sped into the bathroom, where she called a friend to pick her up.

Lana was blown away. Simon had picked the time, date, and the restaurant. And he didn't make a move for the bill? Of course, early in a relationship with any man, you're always taking a "box of chocolates" kind of risk. You're still getting to know each other. But rather than defaulting by fleeing the situation and giving him a free meal, Lana could have whispered to at least rectify the situation somewhat. She could have used a few Man Whispering lines like:

Ask his counsel: "What should we do about this bill?"

State a dilemma: "I'm sorry; I didn't bring my credit card and I don't have much cash. How would you like to handle the bill?"

Show appreciation: "Thank you so much for taking me to such a fabulous restaurant. I really loved every minute of it and the food is delicious."

Show disbelief: If Simon asked her to "join forces" with the bill or suggested an arrangement that didn't feel right to her, an effective line is best said with utter disbelief: "You're kidding, right?" This usually shames a boy who pretended to be a man into handling the situation and letting the moths fly out of his wallet by opening it.

Get Him to Spend More Time with You

Though this may sound counterintuitive, the more you keep busy and enjoy your own life, the more a man will want to spend time with you. Never beg to spend time with him. Simply state how you are feeling—"I would so love to have a good Mexican meal tonight and we could get tipsy on margaritas," or "A walk on the beach would be lovely today"—and then Zip It. If your man doesn't get the message, or is "too tired" to go with you, you can simply state that you'll be heading out with other people instead.

Man Whispering Mantras
Chapter 9

- Men are just as insecure as women—if not more so!
- Flatter his ego in a sincere and real way.
- Encourage him to drop his guard by not demanding he express his feelings or talk about them immediately. Let him retreat to his man cave and talk when he is ready.
- Timing is everything.
- Never attack or judge what he has to say. He's finally talking—so let him!
- Getting a man to be more generous isn't easy—but don't pressure him. He'll open up his wallet as a sign of appreciation—not when you demand that he do it.
- A man will want to spend more time with you when it appears you're having the time of your life . . . and he wants desperately to be a part of that!

Young at Heart

*How to make peace
with the boy in the man*

*"The only difference between men and boys
is the cost of their toys."*
—AUTHOR UNKNOWN

"Man Whispering separates the men from the boys."
—DONNA AND SAM

What Women Want

Most women want to be in a relationship with a man, not a boy. While many men find this notion mildly insulting ("What's wrong with exercising my thumbs on PlayStation all day, leaving the toilet seat up, eating ramen noodles, and wanting to trek around the world instead of settling down with a woman?" they wonder), the female desire for mature men is universal. It's pretty clear, really. After all, who wants to be in a relationship with a pot-smoking, Nintendo-playing, jobless thirty-five-year-old man who needs to be babysat and doesn't have ten bucks to his name? While that's one extreme, the flip side is that even the manliest of men still behave like boys . . . sometimes at the worst of times, when you need them most. So how do you get your man to man-up?

What Men Want

While you see childish behavior as annoying, embarrassing, and, well, childish, he sees it as an innate and harmless part of who he is. If you complain about it, he'll think, "She doesn't let me have any fun!" "She's just trying to control me!" or worst of all, "What a bitch!" They think women are taking the lollipops out of their mouths and sticking it you know where.

The fact is that all men are boys at heart. They all love shiny new toys, games, gadgets, and boys' nights out, and they aren't going to want to give them up for anything, not even for the best sex in the world. (Or, at least not for too long.) And men certainly don't want women to stop them from enjoying this part of their lives. When you whisper to your man, however, you can strike a balance of letting your man stay young at heart and avoid a midlife crisis without shunning his responsibilities or sabotaging your relationship.

CASE STUDY: RACHEL AND FRED

Rachel, a striking thirty-two-year-old freelance writer, describes how she got her man to man-up by whispering to him:

"I have two children and dealing with them all day can be maddening. My husband, Fred, would often come home from work, put his feet up, and tell me that he needed quiet time. I know his banking job is stressful, but so is running a household with two children under five! I got sick of nagging him to get off his butt.

"One day my mother became ill and needed to be rushed to the hospital. I had a choice: take the kids and risk not getting to her in time, or to get Fred to man-up and pitch in. I knew that if I called him and told him, 'You never ever help, and this is the one time I'm asking you, and if you don't do it, I'm going to be mad at you forever, blah blah,' that he'd become immediately defensive. So instead, I told him the situation in a calm and rational voice, and then without even asking him for his help, I just stopped talking. And you know what? He came to a great conclusion all on his own. He said he was happy to leave work immediately and watch the kids."

Don't Pander to or Spoil Men

No matter how much his behavior bothers you, don't prevent him from doing what he wants. However, neither must you pander to him, either. In fact, the more women baby their men, the more spoiled they become. And spoiled men are more prone to look for "where the grass is greener." Why?

In order to mature, a man must go through a psychological rite of passage that requires him to "betray" his mother by leaving her and going out into the world to grow up. Some mothers try to possess their sons and don't set them free into the world to become men. If a mother does that, the son feels as if he is truly betraying her by entering the world against her wishes. The man may try to heal his feelings of guilt about this betrayal by trading one mother for another.

And guess who that new mother is? His girlfriend or wife—you, of course. If you fulfill that role for him, you're only making the situation worse. Why should a man make his own decisions when you are waiting to do it for him? And why should a man ever venture out into a dark, scary place to fulfill his destiny if he doesn't have to? If everything is already taken care of, it leaves a man no room and no reason to venture out and get anything done. That is exactly why so many Peter Pan types love mothering women who protect their feelings and defend them from the big, nasty world. So if you're mothering your man (and keeping him a boy!), it's your own fault he's still acting like one!

Peter Pan type: As much as he purports to be a man in the workplace, at home this sort of guy never fully grows up. He tends to rely on women financially, revels in doing boyish stuff like dirtbike riding or playing PlayStation all weekend, or hanging out with friends when it's supposed to be date night. And he thinks his couch is the most romantic place in the world. He generally refuses to take very much responsibility in his personal life.

CASE STUDY: HOLLY

Take Holly, a twenty-nine-year-old uber-successful real estate broker, as a cautionary tale. When it came to men, Holly's self-esteem was in the toilet. She thought the immature men she had relationships with would stay with her as long as she indulged their boyish delights. She lavished them with presents —an Xbox for Christmas, surf trips for birthdays, and just more, more, and more.

It didn't break her bank (she was that successful!), but it didn't make them stay either. In fact, what did happen was the typical sponge story. The string of immature boys she had relationships with soaked up all she had gave, never reciprocated, and lived like they were single men on the prowl. It took her a long time to finally understand that she was worth more than just being a sugar mommy, and to summon the strength and courage to break up with them. Holly's lesson: Encouraging boyish behavior by pandering to it doesn't lead to a commitment or a healthy long-term relationship.

Man Whisperers Don't Commit to Boys Who Aren't Ready

In the hilarious film *Prime*, starring Uma Thurman, her character, Rafi Gardet, is a successful thirty-seven-year-old Manhattan career woman who meets twenty-three-year-old struggling artist Dave Bloomberg . . . who still lives with his grandparents. The sex between them is mind-blowing, the chemistry is electric, and the two quickly fall in lust. Dave moves in with the wealthy Rafi and goes on to spend his days playing video games, eating all her food, and bringing his friends over to her apartment while she is hard at work. After a while, Rafi realizes that Dave is still just a boy and isn't going to grow up anytime soon. His expectation that she "mommy" him pushes their relationship into a deep funk, and even their sex life quickly dries up. (Keep this in mind: Never buy a man video games unless you want it to be the end of your sex life as you know it!)

Don't allow this to happen. Instead, pick up the signs that the man you're dating is in fact a boy who is not going to grow up anytime soon. Check out the chart on the following page that shows their different behaviors so you know which one you've got.

Can You Turn a Boy into a Man?

No. We repeat: "You cannot turn a boy into a man." Of course, you *can* inspire a boy to choose to start acting like a man. But you alone cannot fully change him. All you can do is discourage boyish behavior and reward him when he acts like a man. Let him know that it pleases you when he steps up to the plate. Ideally, he then will want to please you even more. Unfortunately, a boy (no matter what his age!) has to turn himself into a man all on his own.

A Man	A Boy
Gives clear signals	Waits for you to take the lead
Says what he wants	Expects you to read his mind
Decides the time and place of dates	Wants you to entertain him
Takes a provider role	Gladly accepts your money and gifts
Protects you	Expects you to protect his feelings
Asks you out on dates	Only wants to hang out
Serves you	Expects you to serve him
Makes decisions to please you	Pleases himself
Is up-front and honest	Employs a don't ask/don't tell policy
Takes action upon his word	Doesn't follow through on commitments
Commits to you	Is committed to his own pleasure
Works hard to achieve a high status	Sponges off a women's status
Offers more to women than just his penis	Thinks his penis is the greatest gift
Is in control of his emotions	Lets his emotions run him
Gives generously	Expects payback in greater proportion
Loyal to whom he commits to protect	Loyal to his loins

178 · The MAN *Whisperer*

Five Steps to Man Whisper a Boy into a Man

Remember, whispering doesn't change a man. Say it to yourself three times! But it certainly accelerates the process of his wanting to change. Use these steps:

1. Stop protecting his feelings. Too often a woman thinks that if she protects a man from the big scary world, or doesn't tell him what she needs from a man in a relationship, he will stay. No. That's how you keep a boy acting like a boy. Tell him how you feel and let him deal with it. Yes, this means he might opt to leave you, but if he wasn't able to provide what you needed, you weren't a good match anyway. The more you let him deal with it, the more he will gain confidence.

2. Zip It and let him fix it. Some men need practice making decisions and coming up with solutions.

3. Appreciate his action steps toward becoming a man. You will see him start to slowly take the lead, make more plans for the two of you, pay for what he plans (without expecting you to pull out your wallet), take on more responsibility with life and with work, have higher aspirations, and start to set higher goals.

4. Be patient. Decide how much time you are willing to invest and how much time you are willing to wait!

5. Know your timeline—you don't have to wait forever! If you've made an Inner Ultimatum and the deadline has passed, feel free to share your timeline with him. After all, once you mentally exit out of the relationship, you'll be gone before he knows it. It's better to tell him and give him a chance to do something about it than to leave him scratching his head!

Allow Your Man to Be Young at Heart

Mature men can be young at heart. In fact, this situation is ideal. Mature men can still be playful, joke around, and like shiny new objects including fast cars and the latest golf clubs. In fact, encourage your man to be young at heart more often. After all, it helps men reduce stress and live longer. And yes, we are in the business of keeping our men around for the long haul.

Is He Mature Enough?

While you do want your man to remain happy and young at heart, you need to make it clear to him (and to yourself) that one thing you won't accept is a man who takes advantage of you. If you're not sure whether your man is mature enough to be worth your time, ask yourself:

- What is he doing to cherish and take care of you?
- What is he doing to make your life safe and comfortable?
- What efforts is he making to please you?

If you can think of satisfactory answers to those three questions, he's mature enough. When you feel confident that you are with a man who demonstrates maturity the vast majority of the time, you'll feel comfortable giving him a hall pass so that he can express the boy in the man every once in a while. When you feel complete and satisfied with your man, there is hardly room for complaining when he asks to go on a camping trip or some other boyish adventure. There are so many benefits to a balanced boy-in-the-man. First off, they bring the fun! And he'll help you feel young at heart too. And they know when to turn off the boy in them and switch back into man mode.

A mature man knows who he is because he has successfully come up with solutions when you let him deal with the "problem" (whispering has a hand in that!). He also uses his strength and his skills to build the best "kingdom" for his wife and children and everyone else he chooses to serve and protect. A man only knows his own strength after he has had to demonstrate it.

Don't Make Him Feel Stupid

A man needs to know that his woman will play along and entertain his boy-in-the-man dreams. Or at least listen, instead of automatically vetoing his plan because it's "stupid." These dreams are important because, believe us, it's not really about the boat. It's not the motor home. It's not the racecar. It's his unfulfilled boyhood dream. And on top of the dream of having a boat, sports car, or whatever . . . he'd always had a dream that there would be a beautiful woman next to him too—and that woman turned out to be you! But now all he hears is his dream woman saying, "How stupid!" Oops.

To bring back the fun and stay young at heart in your relationship, it's important that you talk about your childhood dreams.

There is always a solution to satisfy the boy in your man that is both fun and fiscally responsible. Rather than squelch his dreams, work with him to find that solution. Although boy-in-the-man dreams may seem on the surface foolish, they often can rejuvenate his mind, spirit, and heart. He can then channel that youthful and refreshed energy right back into your relationship.

Beware the Boy-in-the-Man Backlash

If you don't let your man indulge in a mutually agreeable way, it might come back to haunt you. Oftentimes when we grow up and reality sets in, it's not always pretty. Bills pile up. There is laundry to be done. Bosses are jerks. There are car breakdowns, colicky babies, and much more. But despite all the stress of modern life, it's vital for your relationship to allow your man the release of being a boy once in a while. If you don't, prepare for the boy-in-the-man backlash! This is where he does what he wants anyway—even when he knows you won't be happy about it. But he does it because he wants it so badly that he's willing to risk your punishment.

CASE STUDY: LINDSAY AND VINCE

One day, an old clunker of a fishing boat suddenly appeared in front of Lindsay's manicured front lawn. "Hmph," she thought, "it must be the neighbor's." But there it stayed all week. Finally she asked her husband, Vince, "Honey, do you know anything about why that rusty boat is there?" He suddenly looked like a cat in a bath.

"Oh, yeah—that's our boat. I just bought it for us."

Lindsay hit the roof and immediately went into her usual tirade.

"What do you mean? You never told me you were buying a boat! What the hell!?"

"Oh, I told you. You just don't listen to me," said Vince.

When Lindsay came to us she was beyond frustrated. "Every time he does something he wants that he knows I'll veto, he says that 'he told me.' But I know that I'd remember him saying that he was going to buy a frickin' boat."

"And what if he did tell you about his plan?" we asked. "Would you have even considered it?"

"No! Of course not!" she retorted.

And therein lies the problem. Clearly, Lindsay did not even contemplate accepting the boy in her husband. Perhaps if Vince felt like he could talk to her about his boyhood dream to have a boat, they could have gotten on the same page about how to fulfill that dream. He might have realized that it would be just as much fun to rent a boat for an afternoon rather than buy one and let the rusty bucket sit in their driveway, creating an eyesore and a source of major marital contention.

How to Avoid His Midlife Crisis

A man who is going through a midlife crisis one day wakes up and realizes that he isn't the hero he always dreamed himself to be. This notion festers in his heart until he takes action to become the hero he idealizes himself to be.

Understanding His Disconnect

Even if he seemingly has everything—a gorgeous home, two cars, two apple-cheeked cherubs for kids, a wife who is loving and still hot, a supportive boss, and a loyal dog—none of this brings a man in a midlife crisis any joy. He's alienated from himself and the world around him. And worst of all, now he's dangerous because he's rash and reactive.

Since he's disconnected from the value of what he has—he places no value on it—he runs the risk of damaging his life and everyone he once loved to the point of ruin. He may act recklessly to try to balance out the unrest he feels in his heart. But the disconnect isn't from the material world—it's a disconnect from his own spirit, his sense of self, and its perceived incompleteness.

Whispering to Avoid the Disconnect

A Man Whisperer can alleviate these feelings of incompleteness and disappointment by creating opportunities for her man to feel like a hero 1,000 times a day. A man who feels like he's a hero every day is likely to keep his midlife crisis away. You can make him feel like a hero in small ways, such as complimenting his tie or sending him a cutesy text message while he's at work. Or, present your man with a challenge that will eliminate or at least minimize his "I have everything; now what?" dilemma. Keeping him busy with his next manly task and adventure answers that question for him by giving him positive direction and focus.

Another way to keep his midlife crisis away is to be proactive about fulfilling his childhood boyish dreams. If he dreamed of rafting down the Amazon, encourage him to do it! Find the time and money for him to go. Go with him if you dare! Remember, doing something scary and adventurous together creates strong bonds. Working with him to pursue his passions is a much healthier alternative to letting his unfulfilled dreams fester in his mind.

Man Whispering Mantras
Chapter 10

- Know that all men are boys at heart, so embrace it rather than fight it.
- Do not pander to your man—this only encourages immature behavior.
- Know you can never change a boy into a man—but you can inspire him to choose to start acting more man-like.
- Don't make him feel stupid—even if he's acting like it!
- Help him avoid a midlife crisis by making him feel like the hero every single day.

PART 4

Whispering for Great Sex and Attraction That Lasts

CHAPTER 11

Grooming
Your Man

*No more rumpled shirts, spare tires,
and man boobs!*

*"I realized that when it comes to getting dressed, men
are a little bit more important than handbags but
less important than shoes. At any rate, we are merely
accessories."*
—ASHTON KUTCHER, IN *HARPER'S BAZAAR*

"When a man looks successful, we feel as if he is."
—DONNA AND SAM

What You Can Change . . .
And What You Can't

Ladies, we know that you want to get your man groomed, looking dapper, and into tiptop, lean shape. After all, if you're going to all this trouble to whisper in order to polish your relationship, you want him to be looking good, too.

We're not saying he needs to emerge with Matthew McConaughey's super abs or Zac Efron's exquisite hairstyle. But if you seriously can't stand your man's hairy jungle back, his wrinkled thermal tops that look like pajamas (or his habit of wearing those horrid white marshmallow sneakers), and wish he'd just once put on one of those damn polo shirts you paid a small fortune for, this chapter has some whispering tricks that can turn it all around.

Sure, every man could look better with a woman's touch. But before you start whispering . . . get over it. Your man isn't a Ken doll. He's not a reflection on you, either. He's a M-A-L-E. With hair in unsightly places. A scratchy beard. And, very possibly, a beer gut. So accept it. Love him for who he is as he is. You expect the same from him, right? On the other hand, chemical attraction plays a huge role in romantic relationships. If you truly feel that something needs to be tweaked for the sake of his health, his sanity, your sanity, or both of your sexual sanities, then read on.

Improving His Wardrobe

You know the old saying, "clothes make the man"? We women often take this saying to heart. So you nag your man (albeit nicely!) to dress better. You tell him to polish his shoes and wear trendier jeans and throw away those trashy cutoffs. Of course, rumples and wrinkles in his shirt are about as sexy as a wet dog—to you. But *he*, on the other hand, doesn't understand what the big deal is. After all, you met him this way, you fell in love with him this way, and you had sex with him this way.

So why do you suddenly want him to change? Why are you so desperate to morph him from frumpy to fabulous? Because, like many women, you likely are attracted to success and status. Hence, if your man is dressing like he is going to get fired tomorrow, it puts you on edge. "There goes my eggs' security," your brain thinks (whether or not you're aware it's thinking that!). So it's natural for you to want your man to dress for success. It helps you feel safe and secure in the knowledge that he's going to be able to feed your children tomorrow.

So you want him to look good, but he could care less. How do you reconcile these conflicting viewpoints? This is no easy task, especially since there's nothing men abhor more than going shopping. It isn't just that they think they're wasting their hard-earned cash on things they don't need—like new pants (when their old ones only have a few holes but hey, they still work!)—when they could be spending it on things they need, like plasma TVs and computer gadgets. Biologically, men simply are not hardwired to be bargain hunters or fashionistas. It's not in their

DNA to go from store to store looking for the perfect pair of khakis. They're looking to obtain what they want in the fastest, quickest, cheapest, and easiest way they can, just as they did back in the caveman days, when they hunted game and brought it home to feed the family. They didn't wait to kill the "perfect" buffalo with beautiful and shiny chocolate-colored fur. The first edible animal within spear distance would certainly do.

This is why when a man goes shopping for a shirt, he comes home with a shirt. And it's usually the first one he saw. But when a woman goes shopping for a new blouse, she'll come home with two new pairs of shoes, a handbag, sunglasses, lipgloss, and a pair of jeans. Oh, and about the blouse? She probably forgot all about the fact she even needed one or that it was the reason she went shopping in the first place! Men view this sort of shopping trip akin to visiting twelve restaurants without ever actually sitting down to a meal. It's just not practical.

"I hate to go shopping, so my girlfriend said she'd do it for me. She showed up at my place with a new work shirt, new underwear, and new designer loafers. Was I offended? No! A part of me loved it. But I think that was because she always let me know these were just things to add to my wardrobe. If I felt like she'd dump me if I wore the wrong shoes, that would be something else. I like her helping me out with my style. As long as she does it with good intentions and a smile on her face."

—NORMAN, 28, ACCOUNTANT

If your man doesn't like to shop, don't fret. There's always a workaround for every issue. After all, whispering is all about offering a win/win situation so that not only does he agree to upgrade his look, but also get the job done with a smile and an open wallet. So follow these steps to getting him to look sharper than George Clooney during Oscar season (George, by the way, is rumored to have worn the same tuxedo for the last fourteen years!).

Plan a Shopping Trip

The first step is to plan a quick shopping trip. Note the emphasis on the word "quick." The purpose for this trip— unbeknownst to him—is to work out his size, his colors, and what styles suit his body type. How do you get him there? First, bargain for his time. When he is NOT preoccupied with a sports game, his favorite show on television, or having sex with you, gently tell him that you're thinking of heading to the mall to check out some hot new brand of (insert his favorite gadget) or whatever your man might be interested in, and that you'd love for the two of you to go together. Casually mention that you can also check out a pair of jeans you saw for him while you're there. Then offer him a reward—maybe afterward you can go to his favorite cafe or pub for a lazy drink.

Organize His Basics

Once you know his size, you can organize his wardrobe and be sure it's filled with the essentials. Every man should have five key items in his wardrobe: a crisp white shirt, perfect jeans, a great sweater, the perfect versatile suit, and a sports jacket. Once you make sure he has the basics, you're on your way to getting him into tiptop wardrobe shape. Plus, once he sees how easy (and systematic!) you've made his life by helping him pick out some key basics that he can mix and match, he'll thank you for it!

Find Out Who His Hero Is

This tip can go a long way toward getting your man to broaden his fashion horizons. Use his hero to emphasize different types of clothing, make suggestions regarding his hero's hair, jeans, shoes, belt—whatever. And then bring it on.

Or, you could nudge him into feeling connected to a fashionable hero that you admire. Say, "Honey, you look just like David Beckham [or other sexpot]!" and point to a photo in a magazine. Or, purchase the latest *GQ* magazine and casually ask him which man he thinks has the best style. Then you can use this person as your benchmark to encourage him to dress a little better—all the while making him think it was his brilliant idea all along.

And then wait.

"Yeah, but my hair is different," he might say.

"Oh, that's easy," you reply. "My hairdresser is awesome. Quick and cheap. And she's hot, too!"

Make Your Own Suggestions

Now that he's got the basics, you know his sizes, and you've pointed out some trendy items being worn by his hero, you can go ahead and do the shopping on your own. Remember, though, to stick to his style. Buy him something that he'll actually like, not what you wish he would wear. Surprise him. Say, "Honey, I saw these shoes and they just screamed your name. I thought you would look so hot in them!" Then when he sheepishly tries them on, jump him. From then on, he might be more amenable to letting you shop for him in the future.

The key is not to be too direct, or he might think you're being demanding, and using him as a pet project. Instead of the direct approach, such as, "Hey, baby, your style is so eighties. What do you think, can I style you?" you should be indirect. Say something like, "I saw this and I thought you would look so hot in it!" Then when he puts it on, gush about how you better not let him out of the house in that shirt and kiss him passionately—or, if you're in the mood, take his hand and lead him into the bedroom. Look at him with lust in your eyes when he wears the clothes that you bought him, which will in turn give him the neurological connection that when he dresses better, he gets more sex. Now what man wouldn't love that?

Compliment Him

Compliment him, but not in the way you always compliment him. Instead, listen to what Hollywood actor Ashton Kutcher said in an article he wrote for *Harper's Bazaar* magazine:

"We want to feel dirty, rugged, and, most important, that you feel safe when you are in our company. So when your guy finally tries on something that you like, tell him that he looks like James Bond or Tony Montana. . . . Trust me, say any of this and you won't be able to get him to take the damn suit off." Remember that the key to a man's heart is in his self-esteem. Don't make him feel stupid for mixing plaids and stripes or flipping his collar up. Simply whisper him into greater style. And reward him for it. Start with one new thing. Reward. Appreciate. Then move on to the next. If you take on too much too soon, he'll feel you're trying to change him—and he'll shut down. Make sure that in your efforts to restyle him, every step builds his self-esteem.

Perfecting His Grooming

Did you know that men in the United States spend a whopping $61 billion on their personal hygiene? According to a study carried out by Packaged Facts in 2009, sales of male grooming products are up 37 percent since 2004. Shaving items top the list of items most often bought, followed by bath products, hair care, deodorant, and skincare. What a surprise: Men are spending more when it comes to looking after their skin. Which means there's hope for your man getting in on the act, if he hasn't done so already.

Here are some common gripes women have about men's grooming, and how to solve them.

Getting Rid of His Unibrow

Plucking one's eyebrows hurts. It's not a pleasant experience. Neither is actually getting into one's car and driving all the way to the beautician only to have *her* pluck some unsightly hairs out of your face. While women live by the "no pain, no gain" and "suffer for beauty" mantras, men are very different. Pain does not equal gaining to them, especially not when it involves a pair of tweezers close to their eyes.

The aim is to get your man to the beautician just ONCE. Tell him it's couples day, it doesn't hurt, and that you'll take him out for his favorite lunch right after. He only needs to go one time to get his eyebrows shaped and trimmed. Then he just touches them up himself once in a while. Compliment him on how great he looks *without* his unibrow, and then reward him with affection, love, food, and kisses.

Cleaning Up Down There

If you think that adding a little more foreplay into your bedroom routine might be your toughest challenge yet, try dealing with the fact that your guy has an astonishing amount of hair down there. The good news is that despite what Sean "P. Diddy" Combs, who promotes the "sack" wax, and uber smooth David Beckham may have you believe, not all women like a man to be stripped, mowed-down, and waxed in places not even Michael Phelps's bathing suit would reveal. But for the average man, a little man-maintenance is mandatory. Getting him to trim may be no easy feat. Broaching it with him, however, is easy.

Here are a few ways to do it:

- "Wow—that's hairy down there! I love going down on you . . . but when it's a little neater."
- "How about a little foreplay involving me watching some hair clipping? Or better yet, I'll trim you. Trust me?"

He might not take to the idea right away. Do not fret. The point is to get him thinking about it. And then asking his friends. (Which is a good thing.) Because with the amount of dough men are spending these days on grooming, at least one of his friends is bound to be getting it done. Men don't mind doing things that their friends are doing. In fact, it spurs on a bit of a competitive nature within him. Push these neurological buttons and you'll have your man trimmed and smooth anywhere you want before you know it.

Trimming His Beard

For some women, nothing is worse than kissing a man who has a new beard that takes off two layers of skin and gives you chin pimples. Women may joke that it's a free dermabrasion, but when it makes the skin on your chin turn red and fall off, it's embarrassing to show up at work on Monday. And unfortunately, no turtleneck is high enough to cover it. So how do you get him to shave so that you kiss without feeling like your skin is being ripped off?

If you find yourself back at your man's house ensconced in a high-octane make-out session, but he's got two-day scratchy scruff, simply whisper to him to shave. Men will do almost anything for sex. If they think they might get any that night, most men will jump into action at the request. Yes, you can literally do this right in the middle of the make-out session. State the problem: "Your beard is really rough!" pausing for a breath with a big "I'm-hot-for-you" smile. Then add your request: "What do you think? Could you shave really fast?"

Most men will instantly jump off the couch and acquiesce to your request. Then, as you watch him shave, tell him how sexy it is to see him do it. It might just turn him on, and turn your whispered request into foreplay.

How to Whisper about His Weight

If your man has a spare tire around his midsection and his cheeks are puffier than a blowfish, it might be time to give him a bit of a helping hand when it comes to getting into shape. But if you demand he do it or insult him about his size in any way, you can say goodbye to any chance at ever getting his butt into a gym. The same goes for his diet. Attempt to stop him from eating another spoonful of his favorite dessert, and he'll put you into the demanding shrew category.

The good thing is that exercise releases endorphins. This in turn makes your man happier, boosts his ego, makes him more eager to please, and makes him want to continue on with his exercise pattern. Start this happy cycle by communicating in the whispering way. Here are a few ways to do that.

Ask Him for His Help

Remember, if you ask a man for his help, his ego is bolstered and he's more inclined to want to step in, come up with a viable solution, and solve your problem. To start the ball rolling, mention that you are struggling to get into better shape and that you'd love his help.

That's right: If you want your man to get into shape, suggest that it's *you* who wants to start a healthier lifestyle. Then ask for his suggestions. And ask for his help in the form of participation, such as:

- "Do you think you can please help me by not having too many chocolates around the house? I need to keep motivated!"
- "Hey, where is that healthy cookbook I bought? Why don't we cook something delicious from it together?"
- "I hate exercising by myself. Would you join me?"

By making "the problem" your own, and suggesting your man come up with a way to "fix it," you get him to join in on your mission, rather than put all the pressure on him and crush his ego at the same time.

Work Out Together

Next, schedule workout times together. In the morning before work, put in a half-hour workout together. Do the same at night after dinner. Make sure to tell your man how much he is helping you out. You'll also notice an improvement in his moods and his overall energy levels. That way, you both benefit from getting in shape (plus, it can do wonders for your sex life). Couples who train together usually lose the most weight because they spur each other on and encourage each other.

Give Him Rewards

Rewards come in many forms, and compliments go a long way. When he is sweating midworkout, reinforce how sexy he is and what a man he is. If you can make it a habit to do your exercise routine together and then go for a healthy dinner afterward, he'll be more inclined to keep the arrangement. We know a woman who told her husband that every day he did an hour of exercise, she would have sex with him. Lo and behold, he lost 30 pounds within a matter of months! Never underestimate the power of a good reward!

Other Suggestions

If you're still at a loss, try one of these unique ideas:

- Buy him a personal training session with a hot female. (But make sure she's gay or married!)
- Research diet and exercise programs that could reduce man boobs and whisper that might be an interesting routine for him to look into.
- Join a gym together and attend exercise classes that he will enjoy too, such as spinning.

Man Whispering Mantras
Chapter 11

- Get rid of all the junk food in the house.
- Exercise together, give encouragement, and reward him with something.
- Don't nag him if he isn't sticking to the program. Simply try another tactic.
- Genuinely compliment him on other aspects of his appearance.
- Remind him how much you love him.

Man Whispering for the Bedroom

Uncover his huge potential to please you (sometimes twice!)

"An orgasm a day keeps the doctor away."
—MAE WEST

"Whisper to get a screaming orgasm."
—DONNA AND SAM

Does Your Man Have His Priorities Straight?

It's not big news that men have sex on their minds. With bated breath, they strategize where and when they can have sex. Men will do just about anything in the hot pursuit of a little action between the sheets . . . whether you've been with him two months or twenty years. Men do realize the fact that women will more readily have sex with them if they put on a little show of romance. Unfortunately, in the case of a man lacking sexual maturity, your orgasm isn't for your pleasure only. It's bragging rights for him.

On the other hand, with a sexually mature man, your sexual pleasure is a goal in itself because he lives to please you. (Imagine that!) So if your man is lacking in the bedroom department or he seems to have forgotten that foreplay exists, fear not. Whispering can turn it all around and clue him in to the many delicious benefits he will experience in his valiant efforts to sexually please you.

Sure, some men already get it. Your pleasure doubles theirs. It feels good for them to give. Bravo! And it feels even better when you trust them enough to melt into their loving care, let go, and come and come again! But unfortunately, these men are the exception to the rule. Which type of man do you have? Check out this table to find out:

Men vs. Boys in Bed

Men in Bed Say	Men Who are Boys in Bed Say
Does this feel good?	Come for me, baby!
I can do this forever.	Did you come yet?
Let me take care of you first.	Suck me.
Do you want more?	My fingers are sore.
Come here, you!	I'm tired. I need to get to bed now.

The Current Status of Women's Sexual Lives

While men orgasm most of the time during intercourse, women aren't so lucky. According to the *Hite Report* (compiled by sex expert Shere Hite in 2004), only 30 percent of women experience orgasm through sexual penetration. And to make matters worse—around 50 to 60 percent of women never have an orgasm via intercourse, ever!

Unfortunately, women today don't want to fail at anything, including having an orgasm. So instead of taking the time to foster real intimacy with the men we're getting naked with, many try to skip the uncomfortable moments of not coming like a porn star and defaulting to the old "just want to get it over with" fake orgasm. Yet that breaks Man Whisperer Mantra #5, "Thou shalt never fake an orgasm." Once you start faking it, it's a long and bumpy road back to the truth.

Another issue is that women are too busy in the bedroom protecting a man's feelings and trying to make him feel like a superstar instead of focusing on receiving pleasure. The bedroom is one place where you need not perform! Sure, you want to compliment your man, but don't forget to make sure you're getting something out of the arrangement too. And don't

204 • The MAN *Whisperer*

bother trying to re-enact the latest porn flick. Your naked vulnerability is way sexier.

Orgasm? What's That?

If you find yourself in a situation where you fake orgasms or are not getting what you want out of your sex life, figure out why before you talk to your man about it. Start by unwinding your current associations surrounding sex and pleasure. Are you afraid? Intimidated? Not confident about your own body? Then determine why you've been lying about it to your man (or putting up with inadequate sex). Are you afraid of hurting his feelings?

ALERT! *Zipping It versus Speaking Up*

Zipping It is a tool for giving men the space and peace to come up with solutions that please you. Zipping It is *not* for avoiding problems you are afraid to discuss. In the latter case, *un*Zip It. That's right, speak up! Use your whispering words and trust the process.

It's just as scary for women to admit that they have trouble receiving pleasure as it is devastating for a man when he learns that his woman isn't satisfied. Yet if he's getting all the pleasure and you're just a passive bystander, it's only going to be a matter of time before your resentment will start to seep into other areas in a passive-aggressive way.

That's why it's time to remember Man Whisperer Mantra #4: Thou shalt Zip It and let him figure it out. Not on his own, of course—with your whispering. Take the initiative to figure out how he can help you. Then use whispering communication tactics—observation, compliment, request—to get your message across. With this approach, you're being gentle and compassionate while still making sure you're clear about your new expectations.

CASE STUDY: MANDY AND NICK

Mandy, a twenty-eight-year-old publicist, had been together with her thirty-year-old boyfriend Nick for three years. She'd had half a dozen other sexual partners before him and truly believed that he was "The One." They'd even discussed marriage. Yet, there was one small problem niggling at the back of her mind: She had never experienced an orgasm.

"I'm not sure what the big deal about sex is," she told us. "It doesn't feel that great. Why are men so obsessed by it?"

Huh!? Was she serious? When we asked her if she'd ever had an orgasm, she said she wasn't sure.

"Oh, you'd know," we told her.

"Really?"

"Hell, yes! We guarantee that you would know if you'd had an orgasm."

We asked her if she derived any pleasure from sex at all. She replied that sadly, she didn't. We asked her if there was foreplay involved. She said that sadly, there wasn't.

We surmised that Mandy's problematic sex life was a result of a major breakdown of communication in the bedroom and that the true meaning of the act had somehow been lost along the way. Sex between couples is supposed to be a special, sensual, explosive, hot, heavy bonding experience. No wonder she never felt like getting naked.

Nick, on the other hand (like most men), thinks he's pretty damn good in the sack. He reckons he can navigate a woman's body better than a mechanic with a sports car. And he thinks that he's doing a fantastic job at turning Mandy on. Why? Because she lets him think that. Mandy is caught in a nasty loop where she either fakes her pleasure or ignores it completely.

Rather than straight-out coming clean about not having an orgasm and asking (read: demanding) him to help her rediscover herself sexually, Mandy whispers to Nick to help him understand her situation. Over a romantic Sunday morning breakfast, she told him that when she was reading a girly magazine the other day, she discovered some sexual positions that spoke directly to a woman's G spot. "How about we try them out?" she suggested sexually.

Nick's eyes lit up. "How about I take you to that restaurant you love on Wednesday night and we try it out then?" He couldn't wait to lavish her and impress her. The excitement was palpable and he began counting down the days till that Wednesday dinner. He did something else, too: He began to research positions and ways to make a woman orgasm better. And when Wednesday night came, you can bet that it was mind-blowingly fantastic. Mandy had her orgasm. How about that for making a man feel like a hero? Nick was up for the task; he just needed to know it was an issue.

General Ways to Improve Your Sex Life

No matter what the sexual issue is in your relationship, knowing the following Dos and Don'ts can only improve the situation.

Don't:
- Complain or criticize him about how bad he is
- Demand he pleasure you a certain way
- Talk about work/family/weight issues during sex
- Resent his pleasure
- Tell him how difficult it is for you to give him a blowjob
- Stop midway through a blowjob, claiming you're "tired" or your "mouth is sore"

Do:
- Create real intimacy by listening to him talk about his feelings or getting him to open up to you
- Guide him on how to please you (more on this later)
- Create foreplay and turn yourself on before you hop into the sack
- Make sexual requests out of the bedroom (via phone, text, or over breakfast . . . that way he'll be thinking about you all day in anticipation!)
- Let him know all the things he does right
- Make life sexy with innuendoes when appropriate
- Remember, men are turned on by visuals. Take care of yourself and look like you're trying to impress him. And do the thirty-second freshen-up before he walks in the door: lips, lashes, and a sexy scent.

Help Yourself!

Maybe your sexual situation isn't as bleak as it was for Mandy, but it could still use some spicing up. There's an infamous saying amongst men that goes something like this: "There is no such thing as bad sex, only good sex and great sex." But women know different. We know that there can be times when sex has about as much spark as a box of wet matches. As a friend once sheepishly told us, "I don't know what it was . . . but it wasn't sex." In fact, it was so devastatingly bad that she told us she hid under the sheets afterward to hide her expression of disappointment.

If your man doesn't intuitively navigate your body, remember that help comes to women who help themselves. In other words, give yourself a boost. Don't leave it only to him to turn you on. Turn yourself on. Psych yourself up. Give yourself some foreplay. Look at sexy pictures that juice you up. Develop a fantasy or a sexual image that turns you on every time, and replay it in your mind.

If it's date night with your man, let your sexual expectation build all day. Send him sexy texts (but not to his work Black-Berry!) telling him what you are going to wear and what you're not going to wear. Women are turned on by situations, words, and dialogue, so build it for yourself and make yourself feel heat inside. Remember, variety wins the day. See if you can get "halfway there" before he even rings your doorbell. While you are on your date, let the excitement build with touch, sexy looks, knowing winks, and heated "I want you" mini make-out sessions. Let him turn you on during the car ride home so your "oven" is all warmed up and ready to cook before you get into bed.

Also, feel free to rub your clitoris during sex while he's working your G spot. The men we polled love it for two reasons: It turns them on to watch, and it takes the pressure off them from getting it "just right." And you'll love it because you'll come more often.

Or, take his fingers on a tour of your body. Help him learn your rhythms. Put your hand over his, and guide him on what brings you to orgasm. Your man wants to please you. If he isn't already a natural, it's up to you to show him how.

Whispering for Other Sexual Needs

Perhaps you have other items on your sexual to-do list that you want to whisper to your man. Here are some common issues and how to whisper to him about them.

For Sexual Variety:
- "Honey, how about we drive up the coast to a secluded beach where no one can see us (wink) with a big blanket and a bottle of wine?"
- "I was just thinking . . . have I ever cooked for you naked?"

For Oral Sex:
- "That orgasm you gave me when you went down was so powerful!"
- "I don't know what you do, but it is the most amazing thing."

For More Sex:
- "You seem a little stressed this evening. Would some sexual healing help?"
- "I'm feeling pretty darn horny tonight." (And then Zip It!)

How to Tap into His "Sexual Giving Gene"

For some women (the lucky ones amongst us), oral sex is something her man does because it pleases him to give her pleasure. But for a number of us, oral pleasure and foreplay are a rare luxury. The only oral sex we encounter is the oral sex we give. Sometimes we overgive in the hopes of getting what we want in return. But that's a double-edged sword, because if we don't get what we want, we feel used, awkward, embarrassed, and unsure of what to do. Then we think men are jerks. But they're not. We just weren't patient enough to wait and get what we wanted.

> **Sexual Giving Gene:** The part of men that is generous by nature and therefore enjoys and derives great pleasure from pleasuring a woman in the bedroom.

Why is it so important to tap into his Sexual Giving Gene? Because sadly, we've heard tons of women complain that they're not satisfied in the bedroom. And you know what? These relationships typically don't last very long. And when these women do find someone who goes down on them, they gloat by saying, "You see! I finally found a man who will do something for ME!" So ladies, either you're with the wrong guy, or you simply need to rectify the situation.

Once you learn how to tap into his Sexual Giving Gene, you'll be experiencing the big "O" more times than you can count on one hand. And the best part is that he'll want nothing in return other than a few words of praise and a nice meal once in a while.

"I love nothing more than to pleasure a woman. It is the best feeling to know that I can give a woman an orgasm. I don't want anything in return other than to know I did a good job."

—BEN, 38, WEB DESIGNER

Five Steps to Tap into His Sexual Giving Gene

1. Whisper the challenge of pleasing you.
2. Zip It.
3. Wait for it.
4. Whisper any necessary audio and visual clues on how to please you.
5. Reward him for his sexual prowess.

Let's look at each step in more detail.

Give Him a Challenge

Men, by nature, are creatures who thrive on a challenge. Since the caveman days, men's testosterone has been spurring them on to compete with other men for the best woman in the tribe. When presented with something that brings out a man's competitive caveman edge, he'll stop at nothing until he wins. To whisper to his Sexual Giving Gene, pose the ultimate challenge: to make you squeal.

If you aren't sure how to broach this topic with your man, pick up a copy of Ian Kerner's definitive guide, titled *She Comes First: The Thinking Man's Guide to Pleasuring a Woman*, which comes complete with diagrams and yes, even a map. Leave it open to the page about oral sex, show your boyfriend your bedtime reading as though you're sharing some hilarious joke, and suggest the two of you try some of the techniques recommended. No man is going to say no to more adventurous sex—but almost every man will say no to a woman who demands it. Alternatively, take a quick look at *The Joy of Sex* or the *Kama Sutra* to help you find a bunch of scintillating new positions that are specifically for one purpose only: to stimulate your G spot. (Our tips: Facing each other on a stool, standing up from behind, and missionary with your legs in the air work wonders.) Men are visual, so gently show him some photos and make some suggestions.

Alternatively, rent a female-friendly porn video or a film that you know has an amazing sex scene (*Wild Things* and *Basic Instinct* are a good start), and casually ask him if he'd ever like to try doing something like what he's seeing on the video. Tell him it appears that the woman in the scene looks like she's getting an immense amount of pleasure and you'd like to try what they're doing to see if it would work on you too.

ALERT! **A Woman's Body**

You can never really ever expect a man to understand what goes on between your legs. So give him a visual map and a guided tour of your anatomy. Let's face it: The clitoris has a whopping eighteen distinct parts to it and more nerve fibers than any other part of the human body. So he's going to need all the help he can get. After a romantic dinner together or a bubble bath with candles, whisper to him that you'd like to give a private tour of your pleasure zones. No man will resist!

Then: Zip It. And wait for it. Those are steps two and three to tap into his Sexual Giving Gene. Yes, it's tough to be patient. But trust us, it's much better if he figures this out on his own as much as possible.

Whisper Any Necessary Audio and Visual Clues on How to Please You

Give him obvious signs, such as moaning, screaming, pinching, eye-rolling, pillow-grabbing, and screaming out the pivotal "yes." And then tell him that your body will also be giving across some vibes. Tell him that when you are feeling pleasure, he'll feel strong muscle contractions, your chest will go red, and approximately 30 seconds afterward, the tip of your tongue will get cold (it's a physiological reaction!). Of course, say all of this in a sexy voice, too, and it will heighten his anticipation.

Reward Him for His Sexual Prowess

This is a great opportunity to create positive associations in his mind. He pleases you in bed: You're in a good mood all week. He spends the time and effort giving you an orgasm: You think he is a walking, talking god. Find ways to bring up and talk about how great he was even after your postcoital cuddle. Thank him and thank him again for being such a generous and talented lover.

Rewarding him for his sexual prowess and desire to please you in bed can become continual foreplay between the two of you that keeps the embers smoldering until the next date night. Tell him as you are doing mundane day-to-day things that you just got hot thinking about what he did to you a few nights ago. Let him know that the memory of him burns deep in your mind and heart, and he'll give even more. Let him know that you sexually desire him even when he's not working up a sweat in bed. Reward him for this and all the other thousands of things he does for you, and you're golden.

CASE STUDY: JANICE AND TED

Janice was in a long-term relationship when she overheard a conversation among girlfriends who were all discussing the merit of the men they had dated who had the ability to "go down" on them for hours on end. *Go down? Yikes!* she thought. Ted, her boyfriend of seven years, had never done that. Let alone for hours.

A few days later, Ted took her out for a wonderful dinner, as he often did, for no special reason—that was just one of the ways that he was generous. When the bill came, Janice jumped in. "Honey, how about I'll take care of this bill . . ." she said sweetly, "if you think about how to reward me later." She then gave him a cheeky wink.

"No, I'll grab the bill, babe," he said, slapping his down his credit card. "But. . . . what do you have in mind? What do you like?"

"Hmm . . . well . . . I'd love it if you'd go down on me . . . but feel free to be creative . . ."

"But I thought you didn't like that?" he replied, a little confused.

"Oh, I do! Should we try?" she said with a huge smile.

With that response, she presented him a challenge. His brain cells suddenly transmitted a huge surge of dopamine (the same hormone released during the chase in the early stages of dating), which gave him more motivation and drive to do something mind-blowing. This was also something varied; something they hadn't done before.

Of course, on the surface, her man was shocked as hell. But his mind was thinking everything over. Nothing happened that night, but a few nights later, while they were fooling around, he went down on her. And god, was he good!

"I love doing this," he told her.

"And you're so good at it!"

Suddenly, she knew what she was missing out on, and was thankful she'd spoken up in a way that invited her boyfriend to do it without commanding or demanding him to do so. Instead, she let him fix the problem she was experiencing and then rewarded him by gloating about his sexual prowess. She even sent him a text message the following day telling him how much she enjoyed the previous night's antics (in cryptic language of course!).

Why Men Fall Asleep after Sex

Don't worry: Your man is not the only one who rolls over and falls into a deep, sedated sleep after sex. When, of course, all you want to is cuddle, talk, and talk some more. If you're confused about his behavior and feel you should speak up about his habit, perhaps you should first listen to two psychologists from New York. According to Mark Leyner and Dr. Billy Goldberg, the authors of the book *Why Men Fall Asleep After Sex*, the answer is biological: "There are hormones that are secreted at orgasm—prolactin, oxytocin—that facilitate sleep. But you have to accept as gospel that men orgasm more than women. If that's true, then you have your answer as to why men fall asleep after sex. And it seems like women don't. If women orgasm as much as men, we might all be asleep all the time." (Which is why you have to whisper to him in order to get your appropriate dosage!)

Unfortunately, ladies, it's in a male's DNA to get some shut eye right after the deed without giving two hoots about your emotional needs. At this point, there is nothing at all running through his head, other than his desperate need to fall into dream zone. Don't get angry or demand he stay awake and cuddle. Just think of all that thrusting, grunting, and sweating—it's no wonder that the poor guy gets tired after sex. After all, he gave you all he's got and if you want more, he needs some sleep to recharge.

The other news is that after sex, women also release the chemical oxytocin, which has a different effect on you than it does your man. As we mentioned in Chapter 7, scientists have nicknamed oxytocin the "cuddle hormone," as it causes women to become increasingly sensitive to whatever happens immediately after the make-out or sex session. But whisperers know: It's not you—it's his hormones doing the zzz-ing. Whisperers also know that if you're still feeling like you got the short end of the stick, that's not you, either. It's your oxytocin that just wants to bond, bond, and bond until the cows come home and won't let you even think about counting sheep.

What should you do? Quick . . . think of ten ways he showed his love this week—and show him your gratitude by letting him sleep.

Man Whispering Mantras
Chapter 12

- Never fake an orgasm. How will your man ever learn how to please you if you constantly do that?
- Don't be afraid to guide your man to the right way to please you. Don't be embarrassed—it will benefit you both in the long run, and you'll forever more be satisfied in the bedroom.
- Man Whispering to his "other" mind is one of the few times when words will actually serve you well. Don't think of it as making demands, though; think of it as giving your man a challenge—and then let him fight to win that challenge. The words you use will turn your man on, because they will create visuals in his mind of what's going to transpire later.
- Reward him for his sexual prowess with praise, words, and thanks. Then he'll want to do it again, and again, and again.

Helping Him Control His Male Urges

*Curb his wandering eye
and his grumpy moods*

"Horny men ogle at ten women a day."
—MARK IRELAND,
THE KODAK LENS VISION CENTRES

"Man Whisper to his Monogamy Gene and it won't matter who he ogles, as he'll be going home with you!"
—DONNA AND SAM

Men and Their Inconsistent Behavior

Ah, men and their moods. We all know that the female species is notorious for mood swings: We get angry, frustrated, stressed, depressed, and irritable—sometimes without warning, reason, or rationale. Most of the time, our mood swings have no grounds whatsoever, other than it's the time of the month when we're (hopefully!) given license by our kind, gentle man to be as temperamental, morose, and cranky as we like without censure or judgment.

But when it comes to the gents and their dispositions, it's a whole different psychological story waiting to unfold. While men don't suffer from PMS, they still have mood swings. And since there is seemingly no regularity to them (versus our twenty-eight-day cycle!) there's nothing to signal us when to pack up for a weekend with the girls to let him brew and stew in a pity party for one (which would make dealing with men's moods a whole lot easier). It seems men can be just as moody as women, if not worse. But why? And when does it occur?

Doctors and scientists think they've come up with a suitable explanation for it all. They say it has more to do with hormones than with how much action men get on the golf course or between the sheets. They've even come up with a name for it, dubbing the condition "Irritable Male Syndrome" (IMS). Psychotherapist Jed Diamond defines IMS as "a state of hypersensitivity, frustration, anxiety, and anger that occurs in males and is associated with biochemical changes, hormonal fluctuations, stress, and loss of male identity."

> "If I'm moody sometimes and not easy to get along with, Trista and I work through it. A bad mood doesn't mean that my wife is the cause . . . *or the fix.*"
> —RYAN SUTTER, MARRIED TO TRISTA AND WINNER OF *THE BACHELORETTE*

According to the IMS theory, men's moods swing from kind and loving to angry and aggressive at the drop of a hat thanks to a sudden drop in their testosterone levels, which affect their brains and therefore their tempers. And just like menopause and middle age, it strikes later on in life.

Of course, while millions of men are affected, not all suffer from it. Some men blame a sudden mood swing on the fact that they missed the football game they wanted to watch, played a bad round of golf, or aren't getting enough sex.

Could He Just Be Hungry?

Other men—like Jill's new boyfriend, a forty-year-old lawyer—can't quite pinpoint why they suddenly start snapping like a bitter child; they just know something isn't right when they do it. It's not necessarily hormone-based, yet *something* is clearly causing the moodiness. Jill, being the detective type she is, decided to investigate.

"I used to get upset when his mood swung so severely," she said. "But then I figured it out: he hasn't eaten all day! Now I simply carry around a bag of nuts and jellybeans with me and when he starts to lash out, I just feed him. All he needs is a bit of sugar and some carbohydrates and he's back to being his usual charming self. Works every time."

In this one area, men are the same as women. If men eat right, look after their bodies, and keep their stress levels low, their moods don't swing too drastically. Encourage him to drop his guard: Buy him his favorite snack and a good fruit juice. He needs the energy. Feed him and give him loads of TLC.

Don't get angry, annoyed, or fight back when your man is moody. Simply Zip It and head to the kitchen, whip up a hearty, meaty sandwich that you know he'll eat (or his favorite chocolate snack), serve it up, and leave him alone. Voilà! He'll come back to you happy as a clam.

Remedies for a Man's Stress

Unfortunately, the solution isn't always as easy as a glass of orange juice. In life there are always ups and down and situations that make men *and* women feel like they're in the hot seat, a frying pan, or a pressure cooker.

If your man flies off the handle, take a moment to discover the underlying issue—the *real* reason he just began screaming at his golf clubs. Ask yourself, "What is going on behind the scenes?" Are things okay at work? What's up with his family? Did he just lose money in the stock market? Once you find out what's going on behind the scenes, you can be a source of relief from his stress by giving him either the space to figure it out or encouragement and confidence in his ability to fix it. This will create positive associations in his brain between you and the solution.

> ALERT! **When It's Not Just a Mood Swing**
> There is a difference between natural mood swings and a man on the verge of physical violence. Violence and abuse of any kind are *not* mood swings. If he is dangerous to you and those around you, leave immediately! Get the help and support you need. Take on a zero-tolerance policy for verbal, physical, and sexual abuse.

The more that you inspire him to find solutions (instead of being an additional source of stress for him), the more he will create positive associations of you in his mind and heart. See your man as confident, competent, and able to come up with solutions to life's problems. Rub his back and say, "I know you work hard and I appreciate it. Look at all you've achieved and provided for us. I'm proud of you. You're the best."

Whispering Strategies to Deal with His Mood Swings

When all else fails, turn to whispering to cope with the ups and downs of a man's emotions. Follow this five-step process:

1. Understand his moods. These are sometimes caused by his hormonal changes or the fact that he's quite simply just hungry. Know that it's not you—it's his hormones and his body making him act a certain way.

2. Focus on the underlying issue. Ascertain if it's work or stress, or whether anything has changed to make him behave this way. But don't probe too much. Just tell him that you understand and you're there for support, whether he needs it or not.

3. Let him burn off his testosterone in positive ways. Encourage him to go for a run, work out, have a small drink, or enjoy a boys' night out. As long as it's all in moderation, let him blow off some steam if you feel he needs it.

4. Consistently reward him for behavior that pleases you. Even though he's having a moody episode, still remember to thank him for something he's done for you that day, or something you've noticed about him that warms your heart. It's always a good time for a compliment!

5. Be the calm in the storm. Once you've told him you'll always be there for support, Zip It and give him some peace to figure it all out himself. He'll come to you if he needs you—which will probably happen sooner rather than later.

More Tactics for Handling Moodiness

Other tips to keep his moods in check include these:

- **Help him set goals.** If he is constantly moody and feeling depressed over the future of his career, his weight, his family relationships—whatever—inspire him to set some new goals. When people take action toward a long-term solution to a problem, their mood instantly lifts and they feel ready to tackle whatever problem was bothering them.

- **Make plans.** If your man is moping around the house, organize an activity together for a few days or weeks down the road. It could be camping or a road trip, a reservation at his favorite restaurant, a trip to the beach—something that he can look forward to. Planning it together also brings you closer.
- **Release his endorphins.** If your man has been lying around the house for days and refuses to get up off the couch, suggest a physical activity. What about a walk? Or a game of tennis? Anything that gets him out of the house, into fresh air, and is a little physical will help him release endorphins—also known as the happy hormones. Make this a regular part of your day, and before you know it, his bad moods will be a thing of the past.
- **Ask for his help.** Set up a project and get your man to help you out. Whether it be on the computer, something physical like weight training, or picking out a new couch for your apartment—ask his opinion, get his advice, and then get him to help you out. When men feel needed, wanted, and of use, their ego is fed and their moods instantly improve.

A Man's Wandering Eye

Along with his moodiness, something else that might peeve you is the fact that he's a serial ogler. In other words, he's checking out every good-looking woman in sight. But you're not alone. A study carried out by Kodak Lens Vision Centres found that men ogle an average of ten women per day for forty-three minutes total. That means a typical man spends up to one entire year of his life checking out pretty women! Women, on other the hand, typically ogle six men per day for twenty minutes total, which, if you think about it, is still nearly six months of our entire lives. The only catch is that we don't get caught as much because we know how to use our peripheral vision. (Don't bother keeping a tit-for-tat score sheet. It's normal and natural for men and women to appreciate physical beauty.)

When it comes to his wandering eye, give your man a break while at the same time using your insider's knowledge of his psyche to ensure that he looks at *you* more than any other woman.

Sports, for example, offer men plenty of natural opportunities to ogle. *Sports Illustrated* has its famous swimsuit issue. Football offers cheerleaders in short skirts and impossibly tight shirts doing high kicks and smiling, smiling, smiling! That's why sports are so popular with men: They allow them to burn off testosterone by watching the game, and ogle at the same time.

What should you do? Let him get excited by the bouncing cheerleaders; there's nothing you can do about them. Then become his cheerleader in life. Let him know that you think he can do whatever it is he wants to do, and that even when he is down and the other team has the ball (metaphorically speaking), you think he can turn it all around. That will turn his mood around—and focus his eyes back on you.

How to Focus His Wandering Eye Back on You

Here's a simple fact: You're not going to get him to stop looking at other women. The key is figuring out how to sustain his interest in you for the long term. Luckily, it's not difficult to make him lust after you. Just give him something to look at.

When a man first is attracted to a woman, he releases two hormones—dopamine and norepinephrine—which give him a sense of elation, intense energy, sleeplessness, and craving. These hormones are released in his body as soon as he sees a woman he thinks is hot. Why? Because men are visual creatures. So unlike women, men can fall in lust almost instantly. Which is good news for you, considering that you don't have to do very much in order to make him feel something for you. You just have to look hot! Oh, and you should smell good too. That's an added bonus that will turn his lustful attention onto you.

> **Lust:** According to the Man Whisperer dictionary, lust is simply the increase in a man's level of testosterone that makes him do almost anything to have sex with the woman he is chasing.

The trouble is that when you're in a long-term relationship, men start to produce a good amount of a hormone called vasopressin. This hormone actually interferes with the dopamine and norepinephrine pathways, suppressing them and therefore making him lust after you less. This explains why the lust wanes after around six months.

The good news is that there is a workaround to keep his interest and his lust hormones turned up on high. You just have to once again generate a little bit of that magical man hormone that will make him go wild for you. Here's how to do it.

Do Something a Little Edgy

As we discussed before, to generate lust, whether you've been together two days, two years, or two decades, you need to raise the dopamine levels in his brain (dopamine levels rise when you're scared or excited). This, in turn, elevates his feelings of sexual desire toward you. Studies have shown that sharing an experience that incites fear—like riding a roller coaster, bungee jumping, having sex outside, or skinny-dipping in your neighbor's pool—will immediately turn your man's amorous attentions to the woman at his side. Just make sure that woman is you!

Spice Up Your Regular Date Night

Whenever couples find the spark in their relationships waning, we suggest organizing a "date night" that is full of mystery, intrigue, and lust. Here are some tips for doing that:

- Get dressed in different locations and wow him with a never-been-seen-before, hotter-than-Eva-Mendes outfit. You can meet him straight from work or vice versa—but don't let him see you before you meet him. You want to take his breath away as soon as he spots you walk into the restaurant!
- Go somewhere different and exciting. Your usual dive spot will bring back memories of boring conversations, mediocre food and service, or just remind you of the mundane . . . yawn. Instead, go somewhere exciting with good atmosphere and great food that titillates the senses.
- Use this opportunity to take your man on a minivacation. That means no talk about work, the kids, stresses, or the boring things in life. Instead, you want to keep things breezy, easy, and sexy. Tell him how much he turns you on. Your man will be lapping up your every word!
- Turn him on. Seduce him with your words. Talk about sex. Get close to his skin and tell him about all the things you've done with him sexually and all the things you still want him to do to you. He'll be feeling lustful in no time, as the brain doesn't know the difference between reality and fantasy. (That's why we get so worked up at

movies and experience emotions as though what we're watching is really happening to us.)

Appreciate Him

Whether you've just started dating him or you're in a serious long-term relationship, you need to fluff his masculine feathers as often as you can. The way you talk to a man on an everyday basis determines the strength of the relationship overall. Smile every time you answer the phone. Speak positively to him. If he feels appreciated all the time, he's less likely to do anything more than harmlessly check out another woman every now and again.

Learn from Him

Let your man be an expert on something in the relationship. Who cares if you already know everything about everything? Let him corner the market and be an expert on at least a few topics. Spark the conversation by prompting him: "Tell me about (insert what he's the expert on). It's fascinating and I know nothing about it." Again, this shows your confidence in him and builds his ego—both of which help him focus on you to hear *more* about how great he is.

Sex It Up

Men are visual creatures. They respond and do things according to the way women look. However, when a man has an affair, it is hardly ever with a woman who is more beautiful than his wife, odd as that may seem. Rather, he is more likely to cheat with a woman who is more sexually aware of herself. In other words, she has high self-esteem when it comes to her body and isn't afraid to show it off. So ladies, listen up: He's your boyfriend/husband—there is no need to cover up or to be shy around him.

This is not necessarily about flouncing around in sexy lingerie and treating yourself like a sex object. Sure, you can if you want to. (It can be really fun!) Instead, it's about looking and feeling your best. It's about him seeing that you look after yourself, care about how you look, and want to preserve yourself, which in turn makes him appreciate and value you more because you appreciate and value yourself.

Know the power of your sexual prowess, and how to use it wisely. We're not saying that you need to be a highly sexually charged deviant or that you need to pull out every fancy move in the *Kama Sutra*. But being responsive and sexually aware and awakened is of top priority in a solid, healthy relationship. These days, with all the tools available to us (thanks to the Internet), being sexual is easy: There are pole-dancing classes, striptease lessons, or dance routines that will be ideal to do for your man in a pair of racy, lacy undergarments. Or just cook his favorite meal naked. Done!

ALERT! *Keep It to Yourself*

One thing that turns men off faster than a used condom is a high-maintenance woman. Excessive talk about designer shoes and expensive hairdressers and fake tan and French manicures and personal trainers—blah! While we're busy dressing for other women, hoping they'll admire our latest designer frock, the men are just hoping for something tight, short, and sexy. Don't complain about how long it took you to get ready or how expensive that lingerie was. Let him enjoy it, for goodness' sake!

Man Whispering Mantras
Chapter 13

- Know that men can get just as irritable as women—it's not him, it's his IMS (Irritable Male Syndrome).
- Learn how to spot his moods and keep them in check by helping him set goals, eat well, and release endorphins.
- Know the difference between a mood swing and an abusive man. Never tolerate violence or abuse. Know when to walk away, and have a zero-tolerance policy for that sort of behavior. Get help and support if you ever find yourself in this situation.
- Know that a man has the urge to ogle and there's nothing you can do to change that. Just make sure you're giving him plenty to ogle at yourself!

CONCLUSION

It didn't happen overnight. But it did happen. Heidi woke up one Sunday morning to find herself snuggling up to James, wanting nothing more than to have her lips right next to his. There weren't any laundry lists of chores to do in her head. Nor was she as pissed off as she had been before, when (what now seemed like a lifetime ago!) Heidi felt that James hadn't been pulling his weight. Instead, Heidi found herself scratching James's back and nibbling his ear. To her surprise, James let the answering machine pick up the message from his golfing buddy. After sweet, spontaneous Sunday morning sex, James got up to make them breakfast in bed. "Where did this man come from?" Heidi wondered.

Then, in a flash, Heidi realized James had changed because she had changed her perspective. It was like putting on a pair of sunglasses that makes everything look exceptionally bright and sunny. Heidi no longer complained about her husband being "useless," because she no longer thought he was. And they hadn't had a blowout fight for weeks. She was actually thrilled when she heard his key turning in the door because now, she was . . . well, happy, since she had begun Man Whispering. And her relationship with James had been good for a while.

Once she focused on being complementary to James rather than trying to be equal to him (which, as she had learned, was a losing battle), everything began to flow. They both were working within their own expertise. James loved cooking, so he cooked and picked out new restaurants to try around town. Heidi didn't bitch about the mess he left after they ate. She now appreciated and thanked James for a lovely dinner, even if the green beans were overcooked. And sometimes, James cooked *and* cleaned. Why? Because he wanted to. Once Heidi learned to be receptive and appreciative of what James gave her, he was inspired to give even more. Not because she demanded it—or asked—but because doing so was his brilliant idea.

When you Man Whisper, the sky is the limit. Heidi picked one mantra per week to work on to change her old habits and practice feminine communication with her man. Instead of keeping a scorecard of everything James was doing wrong, Heidi decided to keep a scorecard of all the things he was doing right. She committed to thanking him three times a day for even the smallest action that pleased her by giving him smiles, squeezes, nuzzles, his favorite food, and even his favorite position in bed. At first, Heidi thought she had to give back equally. A clean bathroom for mowing the lawn. A massage for a foot rub. But then she realized that all James really wanted was her appreciation. In fact, James actually preferred giving to Heidi *more* than she gave back because it made him feel like a big, strong man who was providing for his woman and making her happy.

To help them on the road to Whispering Relationship Bliss, Heidi even went as far as giving James permission to gently remind her that if she ever ventured into the Nag Zone, he could give her a yellow card. (Which he did from time to time!) Now, they were able to laugh about each other's foibles, screw-ups, and setbacks. Man Whispering is an ongoing relationship builder, not just a do-it-once-and-you're-done program.

It wasn't only Heidi who noticed that James had started to take more initiative to please her. Her friends took note, and strangers did too. Heidi told us this: "My relationship with James went from being a cautionary tale to women cornering me in bars asking me how I met such a great man. And I feel confident telling them that he was always a great man, I just had to learn how to bring out his best. Personally, I'm more relaxed and confident. I'm not so tired or high-strung. Life just seems easier when I follow the Man Whispering Mantras of letting him deal with it. Sure, at first, Zipping It felt like I was biting my own tongue until I realized that it's an act of trust. Every time I Zip It, I'm letting James know that I trust him to provide for us and that I trust his leadership. I feel like I have so much more time to enjoy life now that I'm not micromanaging my career and my relationship."

We're here to tell you that you really can have it all. You can have an ambitious career if you choose *and* the romantic relationship of your dreams. And now you know how. So get out there and get whispering. You, too, can be one of those women who seem to have it all. Because they really do. . . .

INDEX

ABOUT THE AUTHORS

About Samantha Brett

Samantha Brett is Australia's #1 sex, dating, and relationship expert. She is the author of four books, including the best-selling *The Chase: Everything You Need to Know about Dating, Sex and Men* (2010). For the past six years, she also has written Australia's top dating column for the *Sydney Morning Herald*, "Ask Sam." As a media spokesperson for Gen Y, Sam has appeared everywhere from the E! Channel to Australia's *Today Show, A Current Affair*, MTV, and radio across the country. Brett dishes out dating advice to thousands daily through her interactive column and radio segments. She currently splits her time between Los Angeles and Sydney, actively discovering the dating scene.

About Donna Sozio

Donna Sozio is a popular dating and relationship expert whose advice has been featured internationally on/in *The Tyra Banks Show, The Early Show, Fox News*, GMTV, Lavalife, Yahoo! Personals, Match.com, MSN.com, *Cosmopolitan, Seventeen* magazine, and more. Her first book, *Never Trust a Man in Alligator Loafers* (2007), is in development as a feature film. She holds a BA cum laude in sociology and avidly develops complementary masculine and feminine communication styles. Donna lives in Los Angeles.

ON TOP

Getting Where Women Really Belong

- Trying to lose the losers you've been dating?
- Striving to find the time to be a doting mother, dedicated employee, and still be a hot piece of you-know-what in the bedroom?
- Been in a comfortable relationship that's becoming, well, too comfortable?

Don't despair! Visit the Jane on Top blog—your new source for information (and commiseration) on all things relationships, sex, and the juggling act that is being a modern gal.

Sign up for our newsletter at
www.adamsmedia.com/blog/relationships
and download a **Month-ful of Happiness!**
That's 30 days of free tips guaranteed to lift your mood!